Fundamentals

of the
process of

SPIRITUAL
PERFECTION

By the Same Author

The Path of Perfection

The Way of Light

Foundations of Natural Spirituality

Spirituality is a Science

Medicine of the Soul

Fundamentals

of the
process of

SPIRITUAL
PERFECTION

A PRACTICAL GUIDE

Bahram Elahi, MD

Monkfish Book Publishing Company
Rhinebeck, New York

Library of Congress Cataloging-in-Publication Data

Names: Elahi, Bahram, author.
Title: Fundamentals of the process of spiritual perfection : a practical guide / Bahram Elahi, MD.
Other titles: Fondamentaux du perfectionnement spirituel. English
Description: Rhinebeck, New York : Monkfish Book Publishing Company, [2022] | Includes bibliographical references. | Translated from French and Persian.
Identifiers: LCCN 2021058414 (print) | LCCN 2021058415 (ebook) | ISBN 9781948626613 (paperback) | ISBN 9781948626620 (ebook)
Subjects: LCSH: Spirituality. | Spiritual life.
Classification: LCC BL624 .E4413 2022 (print) | LCC BL624 (ebook) | DDC 204/.4--dc23/eng/20220120
LC record available at https://lccn.loc.gov/2021058414
LC ebook record available at https://lccn.loc.gov/2021058415

Monkfish Book Publishing Company
22 East Market Street, Suite 304
Rhinebeck, NY 12572
(845) 876-4861
monkfishpublishing.com

Contents

List of Panels

Figures

Before reading this *Practical Guide*, it is recommended that readers carefully study and project themselves within these figures, as if they were a reflection of their own self (their own soul).

Fig. 1a Body or Soul: Which Is Our Real Self?

Our real self is our soul. The psyche is only a small part of the soul, and not its equivalent.

Our thoughts, intentions, words, actions, and psychological states, from birth till death, are fully and contemporaneously recorded in our soul (our real self). Each time we die, we necessarily return to the interworld of planet Earth, where all the information recorded in our soul is reproduced live before those in charge of the accounting. This information serves as the basis of our accounting and the determination of our future destiny.

The human soul and
the physical body. The soul and
the body are like hand and glove.

Fig. 1b The Human Soul Proper and Its Psyche

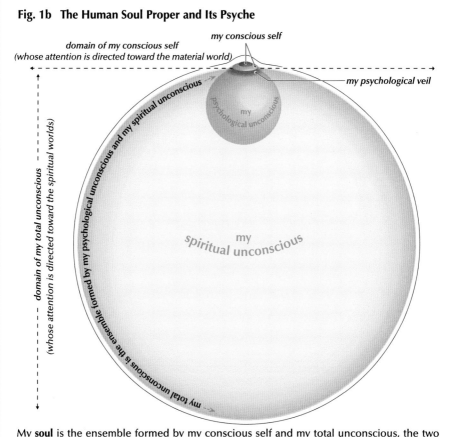

My **soul** is the ensemble formed by my conscious self and my total unconscious, the two separated from one another by my psychological veil.

My **conscious self** is the ensemble formed by my **ego** (my surface conscious self) and my **inner guide** (my deeper conscious self).

My **total unconscious** is the ensemble formed by my psychological unconscious and my spiritual unconscious.

My **psyche**, which is but a small part of my soul, is the ensemble formed by my conscious self and my psychological unconscious.

Fig. 2a
Structure of the Human Psyche According to Freud and of the Primate Psyche

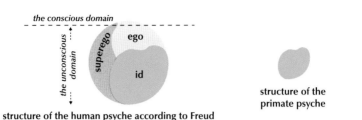

structure of the human psyche according to Freud

structure of the primate psyche

Fig. 2b
Functional Structure of the Human Soul Derived from the Teachings of Ostad Elahi

From a functional standpoint, the human soul (our real self) is a psychospiritual organism, just as the human body is a biological organism. The body and the soul are to each other as a vessel is to its content, or a glove to a hand. The organizational and functional similarity between these two organisms allows us to study the functions of the soul by way of analogy to the functions of the body.

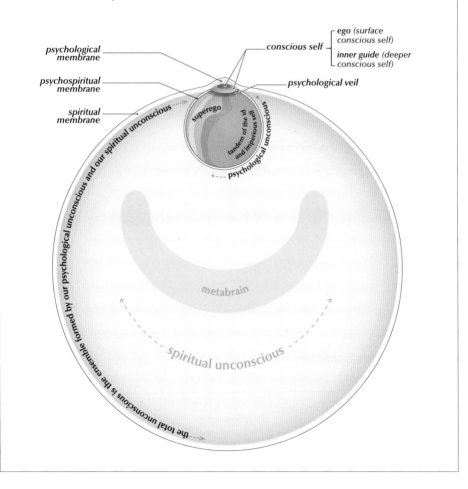

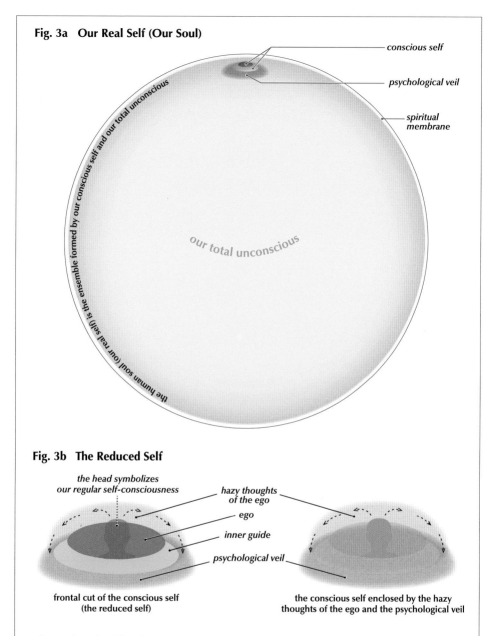

Fig. 3a Our Real Self (Our Soul)

conscious self

psychological veil

spiritual membrane

the human soul (our real self) is the ensemble formed by our conscious self and our total unconscious

our total unconscious

Fig. 3b The Reduced Self

the head symbolizes our regular self-consciousness

hazy thoughts of the ego

ego

inner guide

psychological veil

frontal cut of the conscious self
(the reduced self)

the conscious self enclosed by the hazy
thoughts of the ego and the psychological veil

The Reduced Self and Spiritual Amnesia

The reduced self refers to the conscious self when it is enclosed by a thick layer of the ego's hazy thoughts and the psychological veil. Although our regular self-consciousness, symbolized here by the figure of a head, naturally nests within the ego (i.e., we ordinarily think through our ego), it also travels back and forth between our ego and our inner guide with a yo-yo-like movement. Our psychological veil disconnects our reduced self from our total unconscious (which is in charge of communication with the spiritual dimensions), thereby plunging us into a state of spiritual amnesia. If this state of spiritual amnesia becomes total, we will dismiss the foundations of spirituality—God, the soul, the hereafter, an accounting, etc.—in the belief that reality can be reduced to our physical self and the material world.

Fig. 4a The Human Psyche:
The Ensemble Formed by the Conscious Self and the Psychological Unconscious

The **conscious self** is the ensemble formed by the surface conscious self (or ego) and the deeper conscious self (or inner guide), and interacts with its earthly environment through the psychological membrane.

The **celestial-human part of the psychological unconscious** (or superego) is composed of four celestial-human faculties or consciences: the **certifying**, **inspiring**, and **blaming** consciences, and the **superid**, which primarily feed the inner guide.

The **terrestrial-animal part of the psychological unconscious** is composed of two terrestrial-animal faculties: the **id** and the **imperious self**, which primarily feed the ego.

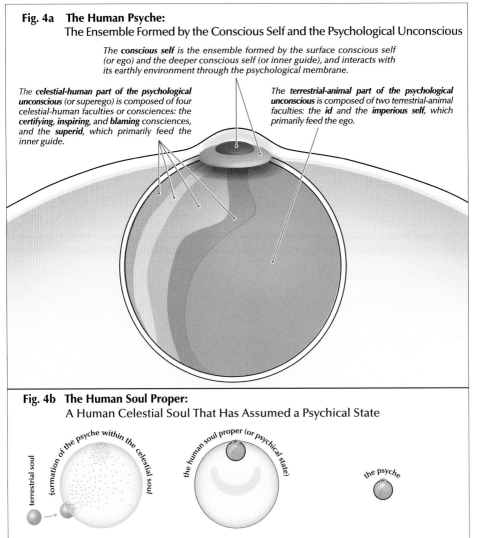

Fig. 4b The Human Soul Proper:
A Human Celestial Soul That Has Assumed a Psychical State

terrestrial soul

formation of the psyche within the celestial soul

the human soul proper (or psychical state)

the psyche

The human psyche, which is but one component of the human soul, is formed in the human soul's "terrestrial pole" by the concentration of dissolved quintessential elements stemming from its terrestrial soul. Thereafter, each time the human soul changes lives, it is endowed with a new psyche and a new conscious self. Yet, the initial sense of self that first appeared within it remains as its permanent identity, regardless of the additional input (positive or negative) it receives during the course of its successive lives.

By creation, the human celestial soul is endowed with a celestial intelligence of great aptitude and capacity. However, being unidimensional—it can only see what is good and positive—it is incapable of distinguishing between opposites and lacks selfish egoity; as such, it cannot undertake its process of perfection. To compensate for these deficiencies, the celestial soul must assume a psychical state—i.e., it must combine with a terrestrial soul and dissolve within itself the quintessential properties of that terrestrial soul's animal faculties.

When a human celestial soul assumes a psychical state—that is, when it transforms into a human soul proper—it acquires a sense of self, a self that bears reason and selfish egoity. As reason is capable of distinguishing between good and bad, benefit and harm, it can draw upon the energy of one's will to transcendence to lead the human soul toward Perfection. If we do not use our reason toward this end, our will to power will instead automatically dominate our will to transcendence, causing us to spiritually regress.

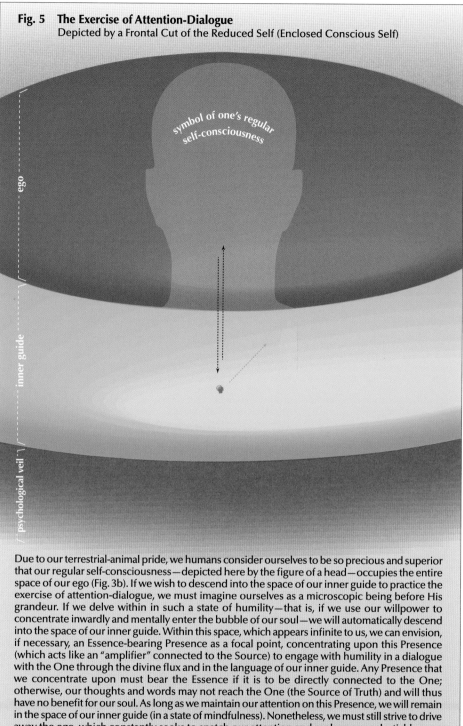

Fig. 5 The Exercise of Attention-Dialogue
Depicted by a Frontal Cut of the Reduced Self (Enclosed Conscious Self)

symbol of one's regular self-consciousness

ego

inner guide

psychological veil

Due to our terrestrial-animal pride, we humans consider ourselves to be so precious and superior that our regular self-consciousness—depicted here by the figure of a head—occupies the entire space of our ego (Fig. 3b). If we wish to descend into the space of our inner guide to practice the exercise of attention-dialogue, we must imagine ourselves as a microscopic being before His grandeur. If we delve within in such a state of humility—that is, if we use our willpower to concentrate inwardly and mentally enter the bubble of our soul—we will automatically descend into the space of our inner guide. Within this space, which appears infinite to us, we can envision, if necessary, an Essence-bearing Presence as a focal point, concentrating upon this Presence (which acts like an "amplifier" connected to the Source) to engage with humility in a dialogue with the One through the divine flux and in the language of our inner guide. Any Presence that we concentrate upon must bear the Essence if it is to be directly connected to the One; otherwise, our thoughts and words may not reach the One (the Source of Truth) and will thus have no benefit for our soul. As long as we maintain our attention on this Presence, we will remain in the space of our inner guide (in a state of mindfulness). Nonetheless, we must still strive to drive away the ego, which constantly seeks to snatch our attention and replace our celestial-human thoughts with its own terrestrial-animal thoughts. It is as if our ego were playing yo-yo with our regular self-consciousness so that our imperious self can disrupt our concentration.

Fig. 6 The New Medicine of the Soul (The Sound Development of Thought)

 Symbol of my imperious self

The two pincers of my imperious self mainly represent libido and the will to power. My imperious self is a powerful psychological energy that is harmful for my soul. Originating in my psychological unconscious, it arises from the activity of my character weak points relating to divine and ethical principles. My imperious self constitutes the main obstacle to coming to know myself and pursuing my process of spiritual perfection. It usually imposes its anti-divine and unethical impulses and desires upon me in three ways: by force, by deception, and by recurring temptations. For example, it influences my common reason and deceives me by justifying my anti-divine and unethical behavior and/or by blaming others, gradually leading me to rid myself of all moral and divine limits to indulge its pleasures. Without the support of metacausal energy from the One, no one can overcome his or her imperious self.

Symbol of my regular self-consciousness

It is through the *in vivo* practice of *living real divine truths* that my regular self-consciousness is able to gradually descend into my psychological unconscious and I can come to acquire self-knowledge. By practicing these truths *in vivo*, I develop my sound reason and strengthen my willpower, enabling my regular self-consciousness to descend into my psychological unconscious along the balanced pathway, the line that separates the celestial and terrestrial parts of my psychological unconscious. "Balanced" implies that I equitably observe the legitimate rights of my body-id and my soul. To avoid straying from the balanced pathway, I align my behavior with the voice of my conscience and divine contentment, and by relying on my willpower and metacausal energy from the One, I remove each obstacle my imperious self erects, without expecting in return any material or supernatural reward from the One.

Symbol of pseudomystical whirlwinds

These ecstatic whirlwinds naturally exist at the border between the psychological unconscious and the spiritual unconscious of all human beings. They originate from our imperious self and are reinforced by negative entities that seek to tempt us and are always lying in prey to mislead human souls. Any spiritual path whose goal is the attainment of supernatural powers, ecstatic spiritual love, altered states of consciousness, or simply inner peace will inevitably lead its followers toward these whirlwinds. Such pseudo-spiritual emotions induce dependency, weakening the soul and arresting the development of its sound reason. Of course, some degree of true mystical emotion—provided that it originates from positive divine entities—is necessary for those who are just beginning, until their sound reason sufficiently develops and the rational love of Truth takes hold within them.

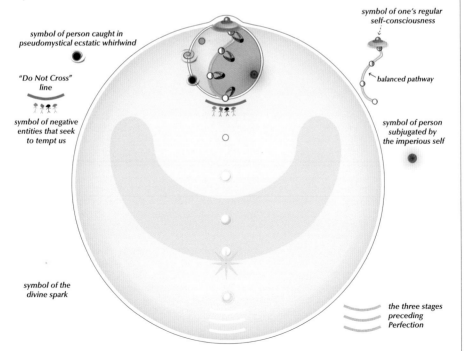

symbol of person caught in pseudomystical ecstatic whirlwind

"Do Not Cross" line

symbol of negative entities that seek to tempt us

symbol of the divine spark

symbol of one's regular self-consciousness

balanced pathway

symbol of person subjugated by the imperious self

the three stages preceding Perfection

Fig. 7 The Inner Conflict, the Inner Dialogue, and the Fight Against the Imperious Self

It is imperative that I become aware of the inner dialogue constantly taking place between my ego and my inner guide at the level of my preconscious and conscious self. This dialogue—which arises in my psychological unconscious from the instinctive conflict between its terrestrial-animal and celestial-human parts—surfaces in my conscious self.

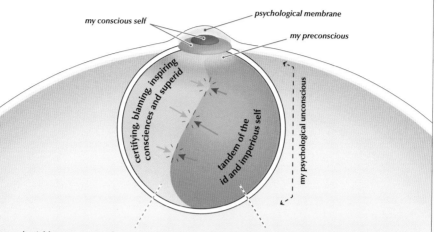

The celestial-human part of my psychological unconscious (superego) is composed of four celestial-human faculties or consciences (the certifying, blaming, and inspiring consciences, and the superid). These consciences manifest in my inner guide in the form of faint feelings and inner voices (e.g., altruism, empathy, remorse, the voice of my conscience, etc.).

The terrestrial-animal part of my psychological unconscious is composed of two terrestrial-animal faculties (the id and the imperious self). The tandem of the id and imperious self manifests in my ego in the form of strong feelings and inner voices (e.g., libido, the will to power, love of wealth, transgressiveness, vengefulness, etc.).

The Inner Conflict

The inner conflict results from the constant and instinctive confrontation between the faculties of the terrestrial-animal part (the tandem of the id and imperious self) and those of the celestial-human part (superego) of my psychological unconscious. This inner conflict surfaces at the level of my preconscious and conscious self in the form of an inner dialogue between my ego and my inner guide. Until such time as one of these opposing forces gains complete control over the other, this inner conflict will persist. Perfection of the soul lies in total mastery of the ego by the inner guide, at which point the inner conflict ceases, giving rise to an absolute inner peace—total bliss.

The Inner Dialogue

A constant inner dialogue takes place between my inner guide and my ego. My inner guide leads me toward true spirituality and the practice of correct ethics, whereas my ego forcefully drives me toward terrestrial-animal pleasures, for it is incapable of properly grasping true spirituality and correct ethics (see chap. 3, "Living Real Divine Truths").

The Fight Against the Imperious Self and Control of the Id

My ego draws its energy from the tandem of the id and imperious self, and is governed by my common reason. My inner guide draws its energy from the superego, and is governed by my sound reason. My inner guide has a duty to neutralize the impulses and desires of my imperious self, and at the same time to control my id to prevent its character traits from straying and becoming new character weak points or flaws, whose activity produces the imperious self. Thus, the fight against my imperious self remains incomplete unless I concurrently control my id to prevent it from supplying my imperious self with new character weak points.

Fig. 8 The Impact of a Sound Development of Thought on the Evolution of the Conscious Self

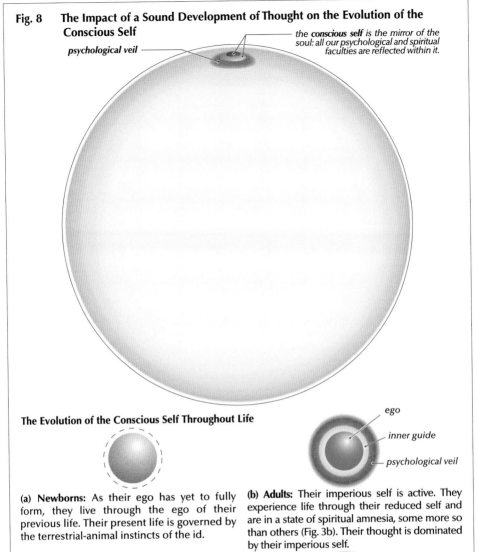

psychological veil

the **conscious self** is the mirror of the soul: all our psychological and spiritual faculties are reflected within it.

The Evolution of the Conscious Self Throughout Life

ego

inner guide

psychological veil

(a) Newborns: As their ego has yet to fully form, they live through the ego of their previous life. Their present life is governed by the terrestrial-animal instincts of the id.

(b) Adults: Their imperious self is active. They experience life through their reduced self and are in a state of spiritual amnesia, some more so than others (Fig. 3b). Their thought is dominated by their imperious self.

(c) Those Who Are Subjugated By Their Imperious Self: Their conscious self is completely enclosed in a thick and dark layer formed by the hazy thoughts of their ego and their psychological veil (Figs. 3, 6). Their spiritual amnesia is total and their thought is ruled by their imperious self. God, the soul, the hereafter, and an accounting mean nothing to them, for they are convinced that reality is reduced to their physical self and the material world.

(d) Those Who Are Spiritually Awakened: They have emerged from their spiritual amnesia; they love the Truth (the One) and are sincere with Him. They have committed themselves to engage in the sound development of their thought. Their life is governed by their inner guide, which maintains control over their ego and neutralizes their imperious self. Their thought is ruled by their sound reason. Their goal is to attain self-knowledge and, from there, to reach Perfection.

Note on the English Translation

F undamentals of the Process of Spiritual Perfection: A Practical Guide
was contemporaneously authored in both French and Persian. The
rendering of the English translation thus faced the unusual challenge
of having to harmonize two original works with minor discrepancies.
Toward that end, manuscripts in both languages were regularly consulted
to ensure the precise meaning intended by the author; any remaining
instances of ambiguity or uncertainty were resolved by conferring directly
with the author himself.

Beyond the intricacies of language, readers of all backgrounds will
quickly come to recognize that this work comprises a condensed handbook
that sets forth a detailed overview of a vast and complex subject—the
fundamentals of the process of spiritual perfection. From the outset, the
author makes clear that the objective is to present timeless and universal
principles in a manner and language that is accessible to modern-day
readers. Naturally, such an approach requires the introduction of new
terminology that was conceived in Persian and French. As is often the
case, a strict translation of these terms and concepts would not adequately
capture the various nuances of their original language. Every effort has
thus been made to identify English equivalents that faithfully preserve
and convey their intended meaning and spirit.

It should also be noted that the frequent repetition employed by the
author to reinforce many of these unfamiliar terms and concepts has been
retained in this translation, irrespective of any stylistic considerations. At

its heart, this work constitutes a concrete and pragmatic guide to the daily practice of spirituality. The overarching goal of this translation has been to effectively convey the foundational principles of this practice in a language that is accessible.

Finally, it should be self-evident that the appellation of "God" in the pages that follow transcends any notion of gender. Whereas the Persian language allows for the invocation of gender-neutral pronouns, the French adopts the standard use of masculine pronouns in referring to God. To maintain consistency and facilitate legibility, the decision was made to retain the French convention in the usage of such pronouns.

Foreword

This work presents that which I have learned from Ostad Elahi,[1] my father, who founded a novel approach to the process of spiritual perfection that he referred to as *the new medicine of the soul*. It is rooted not only in his words and writings, but also in his personal example as reflected in his smallest deeds and daily conduct.

The concepts presented here are not based purely on intellectual interpretation, but rather result from personal experimentation aimed at providing direct access to his thought and teachings. I thus find myself in a position comparable to that of a biographer: To present a faithful portrait of a man and his life, the biographer must render his own personality and opinions secondary to that of his subject.

Extensive research over the years has enabled me to discover the concrete meaning of Ostad's teachings, research that was marked by a constant effort to grasp the truth through an *in vivo* practice.[2] Ostad expressed himself in a language and manner that was adapted to his own particular time and environment. As such, it can be somewhat difficult today to correctly distinguish between what is essential and what is

---

1. "Ostad" is a title indicating that one has attained a level of mastery in a given domain. In the case of Nur Ali Elahi (1895-1974), this title was attributed to him due to his mastery in the domain of spiritual knowledge and sacred music. According to those who knew him well during his lifetime, he was the embodiment of ethics and truth, a human being whose humanity was fully realized.

2. An *in vivo* practice is a concrete, personal practice carried out in real-life situations—that is, in the midst of society and through interaction with others.

secondary, what relates to the fundamentals of spiritual perfection and what is context-specific. The principles that are presented here, however, are universal in their scope: they concern, without exception, all beings endowed with reason, including human beings, regardless of their beliefs or culture. Thus, what remained to be done was to adapt the meaning and form of these principles to our own times; that is what I have endeavored to do as faithfully as possible, even if it has required the introduction of new terminology in some instances. Throughout this process, I have sought to pave a way that will allow everyone to access the Truth and the *living real divine truths* I have learned from him.

My own understanding of these truths has evolved over the years, becoming more complete and precise. Such a progression is only natural when one engages in the process of spiritual perfection while concurrently tending to one's material and family life. Accordingly, any perceived differences between *Fundamentals of the Process of Spiritual Perfection* and my earlier publications should be resolved in favor of my most recent works.[3]

---

3. *Fundamentals of the Process of Spiritual Perfection* is comprised of this *Practical Guide* and the four companion volumes that further develop and explain certain concepts presented here in a condensed format. In addition, a general introduction and overview to the teaching of Ostad Elahi can be found in my book *La Voie de la Perfection: Introduction à la Pensée d' Ostad Elahi*, rev. ed. (Paris: Albin Michel, 2018), which can facilitate a better understanding of this *Practical Guide*.

Prologue

Whether we want to or not, we must all undertake the process of spiritual perfection. Perfection of the [human] soul lies in mastery of the ego.[1]

By creation, we humans are inherently spiritual beings. Whether in our present life or in future lives, we will eventually come to recognize our primordial nature; we will then wholeheartedly engage in spirituality while concurrently leading an active life in society. It should be noted at the outset that the spirituality in question here refers to *the process of spiritual perfection*, whose ultimate goal is the perfection of the human soul. This process must be approached as an experimental science, much as one would approach the science of medicine. In fact, Ostad refers to this process as *the new medicine of the soul*.[2]

As with any scientific discipline, the new medicine of the soul naturally has its own specific concepts and terminology. Given that these concepts and terms are both novel and numerous, a deliberate effort

---

1. Ostad Elahi, *Paroles de Vérité*, comp. and ed. Bahram Elahi (Paris: Albin Michel, 2014), saying 196; originally published as *Bargozideh: Gozide-ye az Goftārhā-ye Nur Ali Elahi* (Tehran, Nashr-e Panj, 2008).
2. Just as the human body is an autonomous biological entity whose health and development are the object of the study of medicine, so too is the human soul an independent psychospiritual entity whose health and development are the object of the study of *the new medicine of the soul* or the science of the human soul's process of perfection.

has been made to gradually introduce them from a variety of vantage points, without seeking to eliminate any repetition. This repetition of certain themes is also intended to ensure that each chapter can be read independently, while still offering its own distinct perspective on the work as a whole. Thus, the most effective way to utilize this *Practical Guide* is to carefully study it in detail as one would a handbook. As for this prologue, its purpose is to introduce in a condensed format the main terms and expressions that appear throughout the *Practical Guide*. Although readers may initially find many of these terms unfamiliar, they will soon find their bearings as each of these terms is further analyzed and elaborated upon in the pages ahead.

The main objective of this *Practical Guide* and its companion volumes is to address the following perennial questions: Who are we, really? Where do we come from? What is the meaning of life? Is there a life beyond this one? And, if so, what will our situation there be? If these questions arise, it is because virtually all of us are in a state of *spiritual amnesia*: We do not know who we really are, what our origin is, why we are on earth, and, above all, what our *essential duty* is in this world.

Yet, whether we choose to believe it or not, our *real self* is our soul; our physical body is but a tool that enables our soul to interact with its material environment so that we can acquire here on earth the *fundamentals of our spiritual perfection* and ultimately reach *Perfection* (the universe of Perfection), whereupon we will eternally live in total bliss. *Total bliss* is a profound state of bliss that permeates our entire being, a distinct state of constant and ever-increasing well-being that is never disrupted by any adversity. Adversity arises from the constraints imposed by *causal causality*; even at the highest levels of paradise, traces of causal causality remain.[3] It is only in Perfection, where causal causality is no longer pertinent, that one's bliss is total.

Perfection is a term that designates both the final stage in the process of spiritual perfection of every human being and a universe unto itself, the universe of Perfection. The *universe of Perfection* is an infinite, metacausal spiritual universe that is superior to both the material universe and to all the spiritual universes combined (the "heavens"), completely encompassing and dominating them. Only rational beings who have reached the stage of Perfection can, by the will of the One,[4] join this universe. In practice, Perfection is reached once we have mastered—through our own willpower and efforts, supported by the metacausal energy of the One—all of our character weak points and flaws relating to divine or ethical principles,[5] and our *sound reason* (the more mature form of our *common reason*) has been transmuted into *divine reason*[6] by the One.

The ultimate goal of every human being is to reach Perfection. Although this creational (natural) right is bestowed upon us by the One, it is our essential duty to actualize this potential right by willfully engaging in the process of spiritual perfection through our own efforts. The process of spiritual perfection in question here—*the new medicine*

---

3. On this subject, see chap. 1, "The Principle of Causality."

4. The One (the original God) is He who is unique and without equal, who is and always has been. He is the Source of Truth, from whom all Truths emanate (see chap. 18 and Epilogue).

5. Just as there are character weak points and flaws that lead us to engage in unethical behavior, so too are there character weak points and flaws that lead us to deny or reject divine principles, such as the existence of God, the soul, the hereafter, and an accounting.

6. The development and perfection of our reason entails three stages: common reason, sound reason, and divine reason.

of the soul—is presented as an educational curriculum for the sound development of one's thought,[7] comparable to the academic curriculum in medicine. This educational curriculum is completed in two stages: the *fundamental stage* and the *advanced stage*.[8] The fundamental stage can and must be completed here on earth through interaction with others. As for the advanced stage, it is strongly recommended that it be undertaken in the other world (the *interworld*).[9]

The fundamental stage essentially consists in examining and mending one's faith (directing it toward a true God), sufficiently developing one's sound reason, and cultivating one's humanity. To complete the fundamental stage, we have a duty (obligation) to sincerely and diligently seek and find *Divine guidance*, which is always present on earth. By connecting our thought to this guidance, we will come to know what goal to adopt in spirituality and which direction to take, what we must do and how we must do it, and what actions we must avoid.

Divine guidance sets forth the process for soundly developing one's thought primarily on the basis of *living real divine truths*. *Living real divine truths* are the prescriptions transmitted by the Source of Truth, the One, to educate the souls of beings endowed with reason and free will (including those of human beings). These truths are described as

---

7. The *sound development of thought, self-knowledge, natural spirituality*, and *the new medicine of the soul* varyingly describe the same process of spiritual perfection.

8. See chap. 13.

9. Ostad Elahi describes the *interworld* as "a [spiritual] intermediate world situated between the material world and the eternal worlds. . . . Upon its death, every being in the earthly world manifests in the interworld with the same form, shape, and appearance that it had on earth; it is the same from both a qualitative and quantitative standpoint." *Ma'refat ol-Ruh*, 4th ed. (Tehran: Jeyhun, 2000), 103-4; translated excerpts cited in this work have been revised by the author. See also B. Elahi, *La Voie de la Perfection*, 90.

living because they bear the *divine effect*. To fully grasp these truths or prescriptions in a tangible manner with our deeper self (our soul) requires that we experience them through an *in vivo* practice—that is, a concrete, personal practice carried out in the midst of society and through interaction with others. By contrast, a theoretical approach to these truths (an *in vitro* practice) will not suffice, even if it is a necessary component of preparing ourselves for an *in vivo* practice.

If we practice *in vivo* the *living real divine truths* set forth by *Divine guidance*, we will develop our sound reason. And with a sufficiently developed sound reason that is bolstered by the metacausal energy of faith (an examined and mended faith),[10] we can come to cultivate our humanity. In so doing, we will advance in our pursuit of self-knowledge (knowledge of the divine spark within us; see Fig. 6) and, as we come to better know ourselves (our soul), we will discover within us the answers to the perennial questions raised above. "Everything lies within us; nothing comes from without."[11]

The material contained in these pages on the subject of spiritual perfection is derived from the written works, oral teachings, and personal experiences of Ostad Elahi, as well as my own observations of how he led his life. Collectively, they present the building blocks for the sound development of one's thought, which leads the soul toward its Perfection. Ostad's body of work as a whole is akin to a vast puzzle, each piece of which presents his interactions over time with audiences spanning different beliefs and cultures. My sole merit is to have gathered and organized these scattered pieces—each representing a facet of the

---

10. An examined and mended faith is one that is directed toward a true God.
11. Ostad Elahi, *Paroles de Vérité*, saying 70.

Truth—without altering their underlying universal truths, such that they reveal a direct roadmap toward Perfection (the universe of Perfection) for all of humanity.

Ostad's extensive *in vivo* research on the spiritual dimension of life and human existence led him to the following definitive conclusions: (1) that our real self is our soul, (2) that there exists a hereafter, which is the abode of souls, (3) that what remains of us and never perishes is our soul (our real self), (4) that all of us will eventually return to the other world (with its multiple dimensions) and will forever reside there with the same self, in a dimension ("heaven") that is commensurate with the spiritual level we have attained, and (5) that the primary reason for our temporary passage through these earthly lives—which are limited in number—is to pursue and complete the fundamental stage in our process of spiritual perfection. As for undertaking the advanced stage of this process, which necessarily involves direct, *in vivo* contact with various groups of souls,[12] it is preferable and in fact strongly recommended that it be deferred to the other world (the interworld), where learning conditions are far more favorable than they are here and our soul faces less peril.

Ostad founded a novel approach to the pursuit of spiritual perfection that is based on the sound development of one's thought. Referring to this approach as *the new medicine of the soul*, he likened self-knowledge

---

12. Aside from human souls, there exist many other groups of souls or spiritual entities, some of whom have a creational nature that is different from or opposite to that of our own and can potentially inflict harm or disease. Learning about these souls through direct contact is an important educational milestone in the process of spiritual perfection. Yet, it is strongly advisable to defer this pursuit to the other world (the interworld), as premature contact here on earth brings about altered states of consciousness that impair one's reason and, in fragile individuals, may result in various forms of psychological disturbances or psychoses.

to a doctorate and perfection of the soul to a professorship.[13] What is intended by *the new medicine of the soul* is that to reach one's Perfection, the surest and most natural way is to approach the process of spiritual perfection as one would the study of any experimental science, such as medicine. In matters of spirituality, everything must be understood through one's reason and *regular self-consciousness* (the normal state of one's consciousness),[14] while strictly avoiding any altered states of consciousness that disrupt the psyche and impair one's reason.

This *new medicine of the soul* corresponds to a spirituality that is described as "natural."[15] *Natural spirituality* respects both the legitimate rights of our body-id (our physical body and our pure animal nature) and the legitimate rights of our soul (our celestial-human nature). Thus, to reach Perfection, instead of repressing our id (pure animal nature) like the ascetics via harsh practices and extreme physical mortification aimed at weakening the body and impeding the formation of the *imperious self*,[16] we lead a normal life in the midst of society while strengthening our

---

13. Nur Ali Elahi, *Āsār ol-Haqq: Goftārhā'i az Nur Ali Elahi*, comp. and ed. Bahram Elahi, 5th ed., vol. 1 (Tehran: Nashr-e Panj, 2007), saying 1152; a second volume of sayings and oral teachings arranged chronologically has also been published (Tehran: Jeyhun, 1994).

14. Our *regular self-consciousness* relies on reason, while altered states of consciousness impair our reason and immerse us in emotions—mostly of a limbic (terrestrial-animal) nature—rooted in the supernatural, a realm whose dangers to our soul we fail to appreciate and whose true significance we are incapable of grasping. As such emotions are harmful to the human soul and lead it astray, we must resist them until such time as our sound reason has sufficiently developed, at which point we will naturally reject such futile pursuits.

15. See chap. 14.

16. The imperious self is a powerful psychological energy that is harmful to the soul. Produced automatically and continuously in our psychological unconscious by the activity of our character weak points and flaws relating to divine or ethical principles, the imperious self drives us to think and act contrary to all correct

physical body, along with our id (pure animal nature) and our willpower. And with the aid of this willpower, strengthened by metacausal energy— energy harnessed through attention to the One or to a true God—we come to control our id. It is only in this manner that our soul, together with our sound reason, can develop naturally and we can advance toward our spiritual perfection. Those who still adhere to the ways of traditional spirituality inherited from ancient times, in which the id (pure animal nature) was repressed through harsh physical and psychological practices, may on occasion be granted a kind of "perfection" by virtue of having endured several successive lifetimes of asceticism or even mortal sacrifice in God's name. Yet this amounts to an "induced" rather than a "natural" state of perfection. Such an induced state can be likened to that of an apple that has been culled prematurely and left to ripen artificially in a depot, precluding it from fully reaping the beneficial effects of nature.

In essence, the purpose of the new medicine of the soul is to develop our sound reason, whose seed lies within the common reason of all human beings. For those in whom this seed has yet to germinate (through the practice of an authentic monotheistic religion), the new medicine of the soul will induce this germination, leading to the development and eventual maturation of their sound reason. A mature sound reason acquires the *acceptability*[17] to be transmuted[18] into divine reason by the One. From this perspective, Perfection is the transmutation of sound reason into divine reason, which constitutes the perfection of reason.

---

divine and moral rules. See chap. 14, "The Imperious Self."

17. See chap. 1, "The Principle of Acceptability."

18. Similar to the process that occurs in a nuclear reaction, transmutation refers to the transformation of one element into another. This is what alchemists sought to achieve in attempting to transform lead into gold.

Those whose sound reason has been transmuted into divine reason acquire direct and objective knowledge of the *absolute Truth*, and, by extension, the Truth of all that there is, commensurate with the station and capacity of their soul.

Before proceeding further, it is recommended that readers carefully study and commit to memory the figures introduced at the outset of this *Practical Guide*. Keeping these figures at the forefront of their mind, readers should look at them as reflections of their own self. In a way, these concepts and figures can be considered as direct depictions of their own soul. These figures represent the structural and functional[19] organization of our real self (our soul) and its psychospiritual faculties. Without conceptualizing these realities of one's soul (which is a psychospiritual organism), how is one to know the object of one's pursuit or the means of going about it? It would be as if a medical student sought to approach the science of medicine without first learning the organization (anatomy) and functioning (physiology) of the human body.

Though the essence of the soul is unknowable, one can nonetheless form a mental representation of the soul by examining the effects that stem from its faculties. Like electromagnetic waves, each of these faculties is capable of being simultaneously present and active throughout the soul and psyche, and thereby of influencing one's thought. In actuality, the human soul exists as an organized entity of consciousness endowed with reason—it is the source of life, consciousness, thought, reason, willpower, faith, and moral conscience (Fig. 2). The constituent psychospiritual

---

19. "Functional" indicates that these figures represent a system of dynamic relations among the different faculties or forces of the soul, considered here as a psychospiritual organism.

faculties of the soul, like the soul itself, are capable of developing and evolving. We have the choice to either correctly develop and train these faculties toward their perfection, or, on the contrary, to cause them to weaken, deteriorate, or even become impaired. To correctly develop our psychospiritual faculties, it is absolutely essential to connect[20] our thought to *Divine guidance* (which teaches *living real divine truths*) and to apply these truths *in vivo*. It is in this manner that we can suitably nourish our common reason and gradually transform it into its more mature form (sound reason), which is capable of correctly grasping both the material and spiritual dimensions of life. Conversely, by focusing exclusively on the material world and developing our mind solely based on truths pertaining to the material dimension—even becoming the best in one's chosen discipline—we will deprive ourselves of grasping the spiritual dimension of existence, and may altogether dismiss the reality of God, the soul, the hereafter, an accounting . . .

---

20. See chap. 1, "The Principle of Connection."

Chapter 1

Foundational Principles and the Divine Flux

The goal of creation is for beings to traverse the stages in their process of spiritual perfection and to ultimately reach total bliss.

If we wish to choose Perfection as our goal—by way of the sound development of one's thought (the new medicine of the soul)—we must align our thoughts and actions with the following foundational principles, which complement one another: *gravitation, opposites, causality, legitimate rights, connection,* in vivo *practice, acceptability, Divine generosity,* and *exception,* among others. Indeed, the direct relationship between the One (the original God) and all beings in the material universe and in the spiritual universes, and vice versa, is based on these foundational principles and is governed by the divine flux. The *divine flux* is a continuous current of consciousness—Divine consciousness—that originates in the radiance of the One. Imbued with His thought, power, and will, this flux envelops all beings and penetrates all things. By means of the divine flux, He perpetually and simultaneously maintains a direct and conscious relationship with every being—from the most minute to the most immense—in the material and spiritual realms, while every being in these realms simultaneously has a direct relationship with Him, whether it is conscious of it or not.

No being or phenomenon in the material universe (the "cosmoses")[1] or in the spiritual realms (the "heavens")[2] can come to exist without being subject to these foundational principles. Nor can any being bypass these principles and circumvent the divine flux, aside from exceptional circumstances that are solely contingent on His will (the principle of exception).[3] Accordingly, creation, the order of the totality of the universes, divine mercy and justice—whether in this world or in the hereafter—all rest upon these foundational principles and are established and governed via the divine flux.

The Principle of Gravitation

According to the principle of gravitation,[4] creation, the order of the universes, and the relationship between the Creator and His creation are all based on *divine gravitation*. For example, the more we advance in our process of spiritual perfection, the stronger our soul's gravitational affinity toward the One becomes and the closer we draw to the Source. And the closer we draw to the Source, the more we are attracted by

---

1. "Beyond this universe that we conceive, there are still other universes that we cannot even imagine." Ostad Elahi, *Paroles de Vérité*, saying 387.
2. The spiritual worlds comprise twelve celestial strata called "heavens." Ostad Elahi, *Āsār ol-Haqq*, vol. 2, 457.
3. The principle of exception, set forth later in this chapter, is exclusive to the One and to those granted authorization by Him.
4. On the subject of gravitation: "We cannot imagine the speed of gravitation, for it surpasses the speed of light; it is even faster than the speed of a memory that crosses one's brain. It is this same gravitation that contains within it the order of the entire universe and the secret to the creation of beings. Even when we seek to concentrate our attention on God, if there were no gravitational force originating from the Source, i.e., if the Source did not exert an attractive force upon our attention, no effect would ensue. Without this gravitational force, no science could achieve its goal." Ostad Elahi, *Āsār ol-Haqq*, vol. 1, saying 511.

divine gravitation, meaning our faith and love for God increase and strengthen. Conversely, the more we deny God and spirituality, the more divine gravitation repels our soul and distances us from Him. Indeed, by His will, the force of divine gravitation can be transformed into a force of repulsion.[5] If we do not strive to align the gravitational affinity of our soul with the gravitation of the One, not only will we not acquire the aptitude to understand and assimilate *living real divine truths*—the essential nutrients of our soul—but we may even turn critical and develop an aversion toward these truths. This is the case, for instance, with those who are dismissive of faith, the existence of God, and a spiritual dimension, at times with pride and arrogance. In reality, it is divine gravitation that is repelling their psyche (due to their actions) and driving them to be dismissive of faith. Ultimately, it is God alone who grants faith, which arises from the force of divine gravitation exerted upon the human soul and psyche.

The Principle of Opposites

According to this principle, all things are known by their opposites: light by way of darkness, love by way of hatred, happiness by way of adversity, etc. As such, one cannot develop a tangible understanding of any matter, be it material or spiritual, without coming to know its opposite. Indeed, the existence of opposites is woven into the very fabric of this world: wealth and poverty, health and sickness, strength and weakness, heat and cold, softheartedness and callousness, etc.

---

5. On this subject, see Bahram Elahi, *Fundamentals of the Process of Spiritual Perfection*, vol. 2, *Natural Spirituality*, chap. 3 (forthcoming).

The Principle of Causality

According to the principle of causality,[6] no phenomenon or effect—be it in the material universe (the cosmoses) or in the spiritual universes (the heavens)—can occur without a cause. Every phenomenon or effect necessarily has its own specific cause(s), such that from any effect we can always come to know its cause(s). "Nothing occurs by accident; even if we fail to comprehend the cause and thus attribute it to an accident, every occurrence nonetheless has a cause."[7]

There are two types of causality: a *causal causality* that governs the causal universe, and a *metacausal causality*[8] that governs the metacausal universe (the universe of Perfection), while also impacting the causal universe that it supersedes and regulates. The causal universe is formed of "matter" and comprises the cosmoses, together with their planets and stars, as well as the causal spiritual worlds, such as the interworld[9] and paradise specific to each planet inhabited by rational beings.

---

6. "Beings have come into existence through the intermediary of causality; to return to their Origin, they must complete their process of perfection." (Ostad Elahi, *Āsār ol-Haqq*, vol. 1, saying 794.) Only the One and the true historical Gods—with the approval of the One—can bypass causality, and even then only in exceptional cases, like that of true miracles. A true miracle is a phenomenon that science can neither realize nor explain at the time of its occurrence. Thus, miracles in each era are relative to the scientific advancement and level of understanding of that era.

7. Ostad Elahi, *Āsār ol-Haqq*, vol. 1, saying 436.

8. Metacausal: all that lies beyond "causal causality" and exercises total dominion over it.

9. The interworld of planet earth is a temporary spiritual world situated along the same continuum as earthly life, only in a higher dimension. "The interworld of each planet is located in the atmosphere of that same planet, and [those who dwell there] are not aware of what is happening in other planets. The same holds true for those who are in eternal paradise or eternal hell: Each planet has its own distinct location, and its inhabitants know nothing of what happens elsewhere,

The Principle of Legitimate Rights

According to the principle of legitimate rights, the Creator has conferred upon all of His creation, without exception—minerals, plants, animals, and those endowed with reason, including human beings—*legitimate creational* (natural) *rights*, such as the right to life, the right to sustenance, the right to reproduction, the right to self-defense, and the right to return to the Origin and exist in total bliss. In the case of beings endowed with reason, He has also granted them the *right to Divine guidance* and the *right to Divine forgiveness*.

These legitimate creational (natural) rights comprise a set of natural aptitudes and means the Creator has granted beings from the outset to endow them with the ability to lead their lives and the capacity to attain maturity. Unless granted a natural right by the Creator, a being can never come to enjoy the advantages associated with that right. For example, the natural ability to fly is a right that has been granted to birds, but not humans.

With regard to certain creational rights (i.e., *potential rights*),[10] however, He has also set forth one or more corresponding obligations that must be met in order to practically benefit from that right. To fly, for example, birds must flap their wings. All beings that have yet to reach the stage of reason and free will fulfill their creational obligations automatically and instinctively by means of natural determinism; as such, barring any impediment, they naturally benefit from all their legitimate creational rights. But humans, by virtue of their reason and free will, must learn

---

unless granted permission. In general, throughout their process of perfection, the souls of beings on a given planet remain on their own planet; only at the stage of Perfection do all souls unite." Ostad Elahi, *Āsār ol-Haqq*, vol. 1, saying 842.

10. See B. Elahi, *Fundamentals*, vol. 2, *Natural Spirituality*, chap. 7 (forthcoming).

the duties that correspond to their potential creational rights and the correct way to carry them out if they wish to practically benefit from them. This includes the most valuable of their creational rights—the right to reach Perfection. To realize this right, they must come to learn its corresponding duties and—through their own willpower and effort, as well as steadfast reliance on the metacausal energy of the One—fulfill them *in vivo* until they reach their Perfection.

Among the legitimate creational rights of beings endowed with reason and free will (including humans) are the *right to Divine guidance* and the *right to Divine forgiveness*. The right to Divine guidance calls for such guidance to always be present on earth,[11] whereas the right to forgiveness requires that God generously forgive, to the extent possible, the countless wrongs that rational beings necessarily commit on account of their spiritual amnesia and free will.

The right to Divine forgiveness is intended as a form of additional help for beings endowed with reason and free will. Considering the countless wrongs that they inevitably commit throughout their life on earth, they would otherwise be relegated upon death to the lowest rungs of the other world and would suffer from indignity and the contempt of others. Indeed, indignity and contempt are among the greatest sources of anguish and suffering for the human soul. As the *human celestial soul,* which stems directly (without any intermediary) from God, is among the most noble (i.e., dignified) of beings, nothing causes it more suffering than to find itself subject to admonishment and reproach.

Fortunately, He is so magnanimous in His forgiveness that descending into such a state permanently is rare for human beings. But like all

---

11. As well as on all the innumerable planets inhabited by rational beings.

other potential creational rights granted by the One, the right to Divine forgiveness has its own corresponding duties. If, in the belief that "He will forgive everything regardless," we do not fulfill at least a minimum of these corresponding duties, we should not expect to be forgiven; He will not forgive us.[12]

We should recognize that as humans endowed with reason and free will, it is incumbent upon us to take the first step and to direct our attention toward God in order to earn the right to have Him turn His gaze upon us. With His every glance, the soul receives and absorbs a certain amount of Divine light. Divine light, *living real divine truths*, and spiritual provisions[13] constitute the principal nutrients of the soul that foster its development, i.e., the development of its sound reason.

In addition to the innate creational rights that we enjoy as human beings, there are also other legitimate rights of a conventional (social) nature. Established by those recognized for their wise governance, these conventional rights aim at engendering order and peace in society. One who is engaged in the process of spiritual perfection should respect not

---

12. "If we assume a state of humility before God and try not to veer from the straight path, I am certain that He will forgive everything. But those who do not exercise self-restraint and do not even try to do so on the basis that God will forgive them, I know that He will not forgive such individuals." Ostad Elahi, *Paroles de Vérité*, saying 332.

13. Spiritual provisions are mainly derived from fighting against our imperious self and performing altruistic, charitable, and devotional acts. For instance, an invention that improves living conditions for humanity at large (e.g., the discovery of a vaccine or the harnessing of electricity) constitutes a spiritual provision for its inventor as long as that invention continues to be used, regardless of whether that person is currently in this world, in the interworld, or in the permanent spiritual worlds. The spiritual credit for the person's invention will be paid into his or her spiritual account and he or she (his or her real self) will benefit as if he or she were living on earth.

only legitimate creational rights, but also legitimate conventional rights (civil laws),[14] for among the wrongs that bear the greatest accountability for one's soul is the knowing and intentional transgression of the legitimate rights of other beings, especially those of our fellow beings. Those who are engaged in their process of spiritual perfection must constantly remain vigilant not to knowingly and intentionally transgress the legitimate rights of others, and, in the event they are unsuccessful, must do their utmost to redress such wrongs during their lifetime. "Knowingly and intentionally" implies we are aware that a certain act is contrary to correct divine and ethical principles, but our imperious self nonetheless compels us to carry through with it and to disregard these principles.

The Principle of Connection

According to the principle of connection, the process of spiritual perfection for beings endowed with reason (we humans included) necessarily requires a *connection*,[15] without which one would be adrift and ineffectual. This connection can be established either through the *chain of Divine guidance* or through *Divine guidance*. The true religions (the authentic monotheistic religions)[16] collectively form the *chain of Divine*

---

14. See chap. 4.

15. "The process of spiritual perfection requires a connection." Ostad Elahi, *Āsār ol-Haqq*, vol. 1, saying 929.

16. A true religion is one that is founded by the will of the One through a divinely designated prophet; such a religion bears a book and is supported by miracles. Every true religion is based on a true miracle, which can only be realized pursuant to a divine command. Thus, only a true God can found a true religion, not man. The miracle of each era is commensurate with the degree to which the mentality of the people of that era has evolved.

guidance, which is intended for humanity at large. This chain takes root in the *Ocean of Truth*, and within its last link on earth one finds *Divine guidance*. *Divine guidance* is necessary for those whose spiritual progress has reached a stage where they are sincerely in pursuit of Truth and wish to reach Perfection.

The links in the *chain of Divine guidance* comprise divine persons—*Essence bearers*[17]—who were necessarily entrusted with a mission by the Source. In the past, these divine persons included the great prophets, who had a general mission to guide the people of their time toward faith and worship of He whom they called the unique God. To encourage and at times compel their people to have faith in God, to respect the rights of others, and to be altruistic, they were tasked with making their spiritual rank known by performing demonstrative miracles and supernatural feats. They actively intervened in the material lives of people, establishing social laws so that they would avoid transgressing each other's rights, practice charity toward one another, and live together in peace and harmony.[18] To compel their followers to constantly be attentive to God, they demanded absolute obedience and established mandatory devotional rituals.

The era of such divine persons is over—one should no longer seek them here on earth. Yet, the basic universal principles they had set forth, such as the existence of the unique God, of a soul, of the hereafter, of an accounting, as well as the practice of correct ethics—compassion, altruism, respect for the legitimate rights of others, etc.—will always remain in effect.

---

17. For more on Essence-bearers, see chap. 3.
18. The laws set forth by the prophets were dictated to them by God in the form of revelations.

The Ocean of Truth

We can surmise from past scriptures that the Ocean of Truth (or the universe of Perfection) is an infinite and hierarchical metacausal spiritual universe that comes into being from the radiance of the One. It is thus a universe of "dignity and metacausal ecstasy," Divine light, *living real divine truths* . . . Those who reach Perfection merge with this Ocean like drops of pure water, residing in total bliss within a universe saturated with love for the One, all the while retaining their self-consciousness with complete awareness.

The Source

We can also infer from these same scriptures that the Source is a whole composed of exalted Essence-bearers who effectuate His will. This whole, in unison and under the oversight of the One, governs the material universe and the spiritual universes (the "heavens"). The spiritual universes are of such vastness and immensity as to surpass all imagination. These heavens, in which innumerable souls dwell according to their degree of proximity to the One, are situated within twelve strata of dignity and ecstasy. The "seat" of His power lies in the ultimate stratum, "the sublime." The closer a stratum is to the twelfth, the more eminent it is in every respect and the greater the knowledge, freedom, rank, dignity, and willpower of the innumerable souls that dwell therein. Without exception, all the beings in the material universe and all the innumerable beings (souls) in the spiritual universes are subject to the will of the One. As the Source itself is subject to this will, invoking the Source is tantamount to invoking the One.

The relationship between God and human beings is essentially one of guidance and education. This guidance takes place through the *chain of Divine guidance* (the authentic monotheistic religions) for humanity at large. But for those who have advanced further in their process of spiritual perfection (i.e., their sound reason has become more developed) and seek Perfection, He steers them by way of *Divine guidance*. Until such time as rational beings come to reach their Perfection, they are in need of *Divine guidance*, whether in this world or in the hereafter.

Human thought evolves with the changing times, yet *Divine guidance* remains ever-present and is obligated to revive (infuse with the divine effect) the real divine truths that are necessary for the perfection of the human soul, while preserving their authenticity and adapting them to the present time. In each era, the responsibility for *Divine guidance* is entrusted to a representative. This *representative*[19] must bear the Essence and be designated by the One, but is under no obligation to make himself or herself publicly known or to divulge his or her spiritual standing. Those who do not fulfill these two conditions—bearing the Essence and being designated by the One—lack any *divine effect* (active ingredient) in their words, which are thus devoid of life. As such, acting on their words does not develop one's sound reason and fails to transform the quality of the human soul into that of truth. As for the guidance issued by a self-proclaimed spiritual guide, a silver-tongued opportunist, or a well-promoted media idol, it leads to the decay, downfall, or even undoing of the souls of its followers and that of the guide himself.

The representative entrusted with *Divine guidance* in each era must safeguard the integrity of this guidance and ensure that it remains alive

---

19. Ostad did not differentiate between men and women, and considered them to have equal rights in every respect.

and current, leading to the sound development of one's thought based on *living real divine truths.* Yet it is not the representative's responsibility to insert himself or herself in the material lives of people, much less to invoke his or her spiritual might to command blind obedience. *Divine guidance* will be of benefit to those who are sincerely in pursuit of Truth and their spiritual perfection, no matter where they live or the convictions they hold. As for the others, this representative will always respect their beliefs, regardless of whether they are affiliated with a true religion (the *chain of Divine guidance*). From his or her perspective, all adults endowed with reason should be free to lead their material and spiritual lives as they see fit while living in this earthly world of spiritual amnesia. It is in the interworld that the Truth will become apparent.

Henceforth, one need not seek and submit to spiritual masters or guides with blind obedience, as was customary in the past. Instead, it is enough to simply seek and follow *Divine guidance.* This guidance presents real divine truths that are kept alive and current by the designated representative. Should such guidance be in a written form, it must originate from a source that bears the Essence and must not have been altered. In every instance, one should consider the specific social context in which these words or writings were brought about and disseminated to determine whether they remain comprehensible and applicable to one's own time.

In every era, the divine effect is present within the representative entrusted with *Divine guidance,* who in turn can impart this effect as he or she sees fit. First and foremost, this effect is imparted to the teachings set forth by *Divine guidance,* thereby revitalizing them. Anyone who seeks to acquire self-knowledge (to come to know one's soul) and to reach Perfection by way of the sound development of one's thought must therefore focus on the teachings drawn together and set forth by *Divine guidance*—teachings that are always adapted to the times—and not on the individuals (instructors) presenting them; in other words, one's approach should be like that of a university student who is focused on the relevant subject matter rather than the individuals tasked with its teaching.

In general, without being connected to the *chain of Divine guidance* and/or *Divine guidance*, it is all but certain that one will be led astray. This "connection" is instrumental in the hereafter as well, for it prevents those who die and reach the interworld from feeling lost at its border and wandering in a state of confusion, not knowing where they are or what they must do, and without recourse to anyone who is capable of helping them.[20] Upon the death of their physical bodies, the souls (the real self) of those who have connected themselves to the *chain of Divine guidance* (an authentic monotheistic religion) and/or *Divine guidance* during their life on earth will not feel lost at the border of the other world (the interworld of planet Earth), for they will immediately be assisted by the Essence-bearer in whom they had placed their faith.

The Principle of *In Vivo* Practice

According to the principle of *in vivo* practice, as long as we do not apply *living real divine truths* in an *in vivo* manner, we cannot concretely grasp their reality within the depths of our being and our soul will not become of the same quality as the Truth. Thus, we will not acquire the

---

20. Specifically, an Essence-bearer that occupies a high spiritual rank in the hereafter and whose words are heeded.

acceptability that allows us to merge with the *Ocean of Truth*, just as a pebble lacks the capability (acceptability) to merge with an ocean.

Note that a text containing *living real divine truths*—if studied with attention and sincerity—enables one to harness a certain amount of metacausal energy that will provide motivation for the *in vivo* practice of those truths.

The Principle of Acceptability

According to the principle of acceptability, as long as a being endowed with reason and free will does not develop within its soul the requisite acceptability (gravitational affinity) to align itself with spiritually-exalted entities—i.e., it does not render the quality of its soul compatible with that of those entities—it will lack the acceptability to join the celestial strata or dimensions of those entities and will be barred entry to them. Even if such a soul were hypothetically elevated to those desired dimensions or celestial strata, it would automatically precipitate,[21] for it would lack the same gravitational affinity as those heavens. The principles of causality, gravitation, and acceptability are fundamental elements that ensure the flawless equity of the One in relation to all beings, both in this world and in the hereafter.

The Principle of Divine Generosity

In accordance with the principle of Divine generosity, nothing but good emanates from the One. His generosity envelops all beings devoid of reason, without exception. But for those endowed with reason and free

---

21. In the chemical sense of the term.

will, the extent of this generosity depends on their own thoughts and behavior: They must earn, through their own efforts, the right to have Divine generosity exercised toward them. *All the good that befalls us stems from Him; all the evil that befalls us stems from ourselves, from our own imperious self.*

The Principle of Exception

In accordance with the principle of exception, only the One and those that He authorizes can bypass, in exceptional situations, the principle of causality. The purpose of this principle is to provide further aid to those beings endowed with reason and free will who are sincerely and diligently engaged in their process of spiritual perfection. The closer we draw to the One, the more He enables us to benefit from the principle of exception. Without this principle, who among us could possibly reach Perfection?

The Divine Flux

The divine flux enables us to explain how the One can consciously, continuously, and simultaneously maintain a direct relationship with every being throughout the universe, despite being one and indivisible, and how each of them is also able to maintain a direct and simultaneous relationship with Him. Based on one of Ostad's sayings,[22] we can assume that the divine flux is like a current of consciousness that continuously emanates from the One and envelops all beings in the universe; in a sense,

---

22. "God maintains a direct relationship with all of His beings. . . . It is by means of this direct relationship that He can establish a connection with millions of beings simultaneously, even though at that moment each of them feels it is alone with Him." Ostad Elahi, *Āsār ol-Haqq*, vol. 1, saying 1682.

this flux can be likened to the infinite field of consciousness of the One, extending everywhere and present in everything. Through the divine flux, the One attenuates the extreme intensity of His light to adapt it to the spiritual capacity of each being. That is how the One continuously, simultaneously, and consciously maintains a direct relationship with every being, without it being instantly reduced to nothingness. Indeed, barring any exceptions—e.g., certain eminent Essence-bearers—no being can withstand the direct radiance of His light without being instantly consumed and reduced to nothingness.

Given that the divine flux is imbued with the thought, power, and will of the One, it fulfills the same function for beings as the presence of the One. As such, all beings in the universe are in direct and simultaneous contact with Him. They all "sense" and praise Him in their own special way and enjoy Divine generosity—all except those endowed with reason and free will, including human beings who are in a state of total spiritual amnesia[23] and reduce everything to the material and physical realm, dismissing the voice of their conscience and denying outright the existence of God, the soul, the hereafter, and an accounting.

It should be noted that it is the One who oversees the application of the foundational principles stated above and modulates the divine flux. His approach toward beings is founded on generosity, and He acts as the guarantor of the legitimate rights of all beings, meaning that He never allows the legitimate rights of any being—no matter how feeble or insignificant—to be lost. Although He determines the destiny of beings devoid of reason, His approach toward those endowed with reason and

---

23. See chap. 10, "The Reduced Self and Spiritual Amnesia."

free will depends upon their own thoughts and actions. If we, as humans with reason and free will, wish to benefit from Divine generosity to the extent possible, we ourselves must earn the right to attract His gaze upon us.[24] If we do not direct our attention toward Him, the principle of causality dictates that He will not look upon us, and we will naturally fall prey to the neglect of causal determinism. With our endless propensity for error, it is not hard to imagine the future that would await us. Causal determinism entails the strict exercise of justice without leniency. No being that bears reason and free will can achieve salvation if subject to the strict exercise of divine justice. Fortunately, even in such cases of neglect, His salvific generosity prevails over His strict justice.

The more we behave sincerely toward the One or the God of our faith (provided He is true), the more we will attract His generosity and benevolence. By virtue of the principle of exception, our sincerity results in Him being more watchful over us: He becomes more forgiving of our mistakes, helps to further mitigate their consequences, and brings more bounty to our lives. As a result of this sincerity, He also connects us to *Divine guidance*, thereby steering us toward our ultimate goal (Perfection) and watching over us so we don't go astray. And on those countless occasions that we nonetheless do go astray, He will set us back on track.

A sincere person is one who wholeheartedly desires to draw closer to Him and who acts with rectitude and honesty, loyalty and selflessness, in relation to Him. Such a person strives to prefer God's contentment to that of his or her own ego,[25] even if it is self-imposed. Rectitude stands

---

24. "[T]he cable is always connected [to the power plant], but the switch must be activated to establish the current." Ostad Elahi, *Āsār ol-Haqq*, vol. 2, saying 278.
25. The ego is in direct contact with one's environment and is the site where the

in opposition to hypocrisy and deceit; it implies that our words mirror what lies in our heart. Honesty is to want for others the same good that we would want for ourselves, and to not want for them that which we would deem bad for ourselves. Loyalty is to remain faithful and to not abandon those we befriend (especially in times of distress or weakness). For example, one remains true to one's faith in God, even if that faith is not shared by those around us. Selflessness (especially in relation to God) is being able to renounce one's ego when needed, such as sincerely setting aside our ego in service of a friend (or a soldier, for example, who comes to the aid of a wounded fellow warrior). Those who persist in such behavior will in time reach a point where they truly love God. And if they continue further still, they will come to love Him more than they love themselves. Once they have reached such a state, they will leave behind their ego and will seek nothing but His contentment.

---

tandem of the id and imperious self expresses itself (Figs. 2 and 4). This tandem assumes control of our common reason and converts it into its own spokesperson. The id, the imperious self, and our common reason thus collectively carry out the functions of the ego. The ego corresponds to what Ostad Elahi calls *nafs* in Persian, and the imperious self to what he calls *nafs-e ammāreh*. See Ostad Elahi, *Paroles de Vérité*, saying 85.

Chapter 2

Sound Reason and the Rational Love of Truth

*Our spiritual development is measured by
the development of our sound reason.*

T he impulse to worship and the impulse to seek truth are part of the
primordial nature of all human beings. The first impulse awakens
within us the desire to worship the sublime; its purpose is to engender
faith and to steer us toward that which we refer to as "God." The second
impulse awakens our scientific curiosity and drives us to know the truth
behind any object or phenomenon that captures our attention, as well
as to understand its function and reason for being. Its main purpose,
however, is to create within us the impetus to know the Truth[1] and to
practice *living real divine truths*, which are among the essential nutrients
for the perfection of our soul.

There are some who channel these two impulses toward the knowledge
of physical matter and nature, while others express them through a
penchant for theological discourse (*in vitro* knowledge). But the vast
majority are merely absorbed in the preoccupations of daily life, focusing
their impulse to worship on manmade idols, especially media icons.
And if they do happen to turn to God or spirituality, all too often they
content themselves with uncritically adopting the beliefs and practices

---

1. See chap. 19, "What is Meant by 'Truth'?"

of their ancestors. Nonetheless, there will always be those who strive to channel these twin impulses toward *in vivo* knowledge of the Truth and of *living real divine truths*. They embrace Perfection as their ultimate goal and consider the material and spiritual realm to be inseparable and indispensable to one another. While they lead an otherwise normal existence in society and earn their livelihood through their own efforts, they diligently strive to integrate their spiritual pursuit into their daily lives.

In principle, once our attention is seriously drawn toward God and spirituality, the impulse to worship and the impulse to seek truth become activated within us. The impulse to worship engenders a *primary divine love* or "faith" in God,[2] whereas the impulse to seek truth leads us to ask and explore such questions as: What is the truth of our being? Who is God? What is the soul? Is there a hereafter beyond this world and, if so, what circumstances await us there?

Faith in God is an emotion, an intuition, an impulse that only He grants,[3] but it is up to us to examine and mend it, to solidify it within ourselves, and to develop it. What is meant by examining and mending our faith is to exercise diligence to ensure that the object of our faith is a true God (bearing the thought, power, and will of the One);[4] otherwise, not only will our faith have no benefit for our soul, but it may even

---

2. The human celestial soul innately feels a strong gravitational attraction toward its Origin, the One (the original God). It is this same innate attraction that awakens and activates the faith in God that lies dormant within each of us. By virtue of their celestial soul, human beings are innately spiritual.

3. "As long as He does not cast His gaze and light upon one's heart, one will not find faith nor be drawn to Him." Ostad Elahi, *Āsār ol-Haqq*, vol. 2, 418.

4. There are many imaginary gods that are deemed authentic due to our insufficient knowledge of spirituality.

prove detrimental. Faith, when it is right (correct faith) and sufficiently developed,[5] soothes the heart and engenders optimism and hope in the future. In its mature state, it becomes inscribed in the soul and stays with us indefinitely in our future lives.

For the majority of people, their faith—whether fostered during childhood in their present lives or inherited from their past lives—currently remains in a dormant (inactive) state. To awaken and activate their faith, all they need is a favorable environment and/or a glance from the One. One of the main duties (missions) of the authentic prophets and saints of the past was to awaken and activate this faith in God. Faith, supported by the impulse to seek truth, predisposes one to more readily embrace the process of soundly developing one's thought and to develop one's sound reason through the practice of *living real divine truths* set forth by *Divine guidance*.

Sound Reason

Sound reason, a more mature form of common reason, is capable of correctly grasping the spiritual dimension of life in addition to its material dimension. The seed of sound reason is placed within the common reason of all human beings at creation, but it is each person's own responsibility to see to its germination and development. Reason is an intellectual faculty that enables comprehension and discernment, allowing us to distinguish truth from falsehood and to discern the relationship between

---

5. There are various stages in the evolution of faith: Faith in the right source (faith in a true God), faith that is sincere, faith that is whole (complete), and the rational love of Truth. A person whose faith in a true God is whole no longer doubts the existence of God or the hereafter, and practices His prescriptions earnestly and sincerely.

cause and effect, benefit and harm, goodness and evil, etc. From the outset, human beings on earth are endowed with common reason.

In principle, nothing in creation is either mature or perfect at its inception, and our common reason is no exception to this rule. Thus, just as we develop our common reason through study and personal experience, we have a duty, through the sound development of our thought, to sufficiently develop the seed of our sound reason (found within our common reason) in order to grasp the spiritual dimension of matters as well. We should not expect our sound reason to develop spontaneously; it will not do so. Rather, we ourselves must tend to its development. As such, it is possible to develop one's common reason to the point of reaching the pinnacle of a given discipline, and yet to simultaneously neglect the development of one's sound reason. In such a case, one would remain incapable of correctly discerning the spiritual dimension of life and *living real divine truths*, whose comprehension pertains to the domain of sound reason.

To develop our sound reason, we must begin by practicing, in a diligent and *in vivo* manner, correct divine and ethical principles (which are included among *living real divine truths*). As our sound reason develops, our faith (primary divine love) evolves and transforms into a *rational love of Truth*, a love that stems from our sound reason. Thereafter, a virtuous cycle emerges between our rational love of Truth and the development of our sound reason: The more our sound reason develops, the stronger our rational love of Truth becomes, and the stronger our rational love of Truth becomes, the more our sound reason develops. Sound reason, thus bolstered by the energy of our rational love of Truth, gradually and steadily leads us along our process of spiritual perfection.

The Rational Love of Truth

The rational love of Truth and of *living real divine truths* is analogous to the rational love felt by scientists for the truths of their discipline, with the difference that for the latter, their love is inspired by their common reason and is focused solely on material realities. The difference between primary divine love (faith) and the rational love of Truth is that the former is only a sentiment or intuition, an emotion that is engendered by the impulse to worship and thus prone to error. By contrast, insofar as the rational love of Truth stems from our sound reason, it is also accompanied by the ability to discern Truth and *living real divine truths*. The stronger our rational love of Truth (which stems from sound reason) becomes, the less material preoccupations and concerns weigh on our psyche; not only does such love increase our sense of peace and inner freedom, but it also awakens empathy and compassion within us.

A person whose sound reason is sufficiently developed is drawn neither toward futile material pursuits (worldly activities and efforts that add no positive value to one's life here or in the hereafter), nor toward futile spiritual pursuits (religious or spiritual beliefs and prescriptions that contribute nothing to the development of one's sound reason or to the acquisition of spiritual provisions). Such a person, moreover, is not deceived by the philosophical sophistry or theatrics of the many misguided spiritual paths and empty (soulless) religions.[6]

---

6. A "soulless" religion is one that is either manmade (a false religion) or was at one time authentic in that it bore the divine effect (its soul), but has since lost that effect due to human interference. Such a religion is devoid of a soul and thus defunct; its practice is of no benefit to the soul (see chap. 3).

The Sensorial Method and the Rational Method

Love (emotional drive) and reason (comprehension and discernment) are both necessary for our process of spiritual perfection. Indeed, this process can be approached in two different ways: one that relies primarily on emotion (the *sensorial method*), or one that relies primarily on sound reason (the *rational method*).

In the sensorial method (traditional spirituality), the primary emphasis is on faith, sentiment, self-sacrifice (to the point of giving one's life), as well as the pursuit of miracles, wonders, and states of ecstatic mystical love. By contrast, the primary emphasis in the rational method (natural spirituality, or the new medicine of the soul) is on the development of sound reason and the rational love of Truth. The rational love of Truth engenders an enduring motivation to understand the Truth as well as *living real divine truths*. The more we advance in our process of spiritual perfection and draw closer to the ultimate goal (Perfection), the more this love is strengthened within us.

One can gather from Ostad's teachings that traditional spirituality (the sensorial method), though more attractive at the outset, is fraught with peril and the danger of being led astray. It is ill-adapted to the social circumstances and intellectual development of today's human beings and those of future generations; it can even prove harmful to the soul. That is why after pursuing traditional spirituality to its zenith, Ostad set forth and advised the adoption of the rational method, which he called *the new medicine of the soul*. This method favors the development of sound reason and the rational love of Truth. In spite of being less appealing than the sensorial method at first, it can more naturally and reliably guide us toward Perfection, with far less risk of straying off course.

The rational love of Truth differs in many respects from forms of love that are causal and mystical in nature. Such forms of *casual mystical love* are imbued to varying degrees with desires of the ego, but are cloaked in a spiritual guise. Long praised by society at large, they have often been perceived as the essential purpose of spirituality. As these forms of causal mystical love generally bear imprints of the emotional brain or limbic system,[7] they can also be referred to as "limbic mystical love."

These forms of love act like potent psychedelic agents that stir the ego, especially the imperious self, plunging one into ecstatic states of altered consciousness—often accompanied by delirium and delusions of grandeur—that impair one's discernment. As such, that which we perceive during these altered states of consciousness cannot be deemed reliable and presents a danger of leading one astray from the Truth. Thus, prudence dictates that we avoid such forms of limbic mystical love, and instead wait until our sound reason has sufficiently developed and the rational love of Truth has emerged within us. Thereafter, as this rational love of Truth grows stronger, the lure of mystical love will begin to fade.

To distinguish which form of love drives us, we must engage in some self-reflection and analyze our psyche to identify the imprints of concealed desires of the ego within us—that is, desires that stem from our libido[8] and will to power, but are expressed in the guise of spiritual

---

7. The limbic system consists of a set of neurological structures related to the primitive brain. Centrally located within the brain, it fulfills a primary function in the processing of emotions, including those of causal or limbic mystical love. The use of the term "limbic" is intended to emphasize the active role of the tandem of the id and imperious self in these types of ecstatic states.

8. Libido: A fundamental psychological energy that ceaselessly drives us to seek insatiable sensual pleasures. At its core is the sexual impulse, though it also manifests through other impulses and desires—the pursuit of wealth and celebrity, inordinate attachment to worldly attractions, the desire for revenge, etc.

justifications. To preserve the natural balance between body and mind while remaining wary of the deceptive pseudospiritual justifications of our imperious self, we must respect the legitimate forms of limbic love[9] that stem from our id (our pure animal nature).

In the more advanced stages of the process of spiritual perfection wherein one is able to achieve complete control over the ego, one naturally enters the stage of becoming "annihilated in God."[10] In this state, an ecstatic spiritual love for God spontaneously blossoms within and overtakes one's thought, leaving no room for causal (limbic) mystical love.[11] It is this kind of love during the final stages of the process of spiritual perfection that enables one to soar toward the ultimate goal (Perfection).

Yet actually reaching the ultimate goal of Perfection—which corresponds to the transmutation of one's sound reason into divine reason—is solely dependent upon His will. At the level of Perfection, one comes to know the Truth firsthand, and from there, the truth of all things within one's field of perception. Commensurate with the station and capacity of one's soul, no point in creation remains obscure; one's

---

9. These legitimate forms of limbic love include the love of a parent for a child, the love for a spouse, and more generally the natural love of life (love of the arts, beauty, nature, etc.). Such love is beneficial and even necessary for the psyche and soul, as long as it is not excessive or misplaced, meaning that it does not turn into an obsession or a causal charge (see "Causal Charges," chap. 11). In the context of natural spirituality, it is essential that we provide our psyche with legitimate forms of healthy recreation, for a weary and agitated psyche is ineffective for the process of spiritual perfection.

10. A reference to the mystical term *fanā' fī-Allāh* (annihilation in God), the final stage in the quest to achieve union with God, wherein one's own will ceases to exist and one loses oneself in the love of God.

11. "Love, no matter its form, is never devoid of the ego." Unpublished letter by Ostad Elahi (August 7, 1955).

love also becomes perfect. There is no greater pleasure or joy than to grasp a *living real divine truth*, nor does any love touch or elate us more profoundly and enduringly than the rational love of Truth.

Indeed, therein lies the goal of creation: for each being to complete the stages in its process of spiritual perfection and to ultimately reach Perfection (the universe of Perfection), where, fully liberated from the burdensome constraints of causal causality, it will forever reside in total bliss.

Chapter 3

Truth, Essence-Bearers, Divine Light, Living Real Divine Truths

Truth

Truth is none other than the One (the original God). The One is pure Essence and invisible, from whom all Truths emanate. Although the nature of this Essence is unknowable to beings, they can nonetheless become cognizant of it through its effects. From the radiance of this Essence emanates the *Ocean of Truth* (the universe of Perfection), which is like an infinite metacausal universe composed of Divine light, *living real divine truths*, and countless other delightful and ineffable wonders.

Truth and Essence are not tangible through words alone; they must be grasped through the senses of the soul.[1] Among those who fail to spiritually grasp the Truth (Essence) or *living real divine truths* beyond appearances, some will altogether turn their backs on God, religion, and true spirituality, while those who are susceptible to staged theatrics will become easy prey for the numerous philosophical movements, self-promoting and ego-flattering delusive spiritual paths, or novel

---

1. In response to the question of whether God can be seen, Malak Jan replies: "Yes, we can see Him, but with the eyes of the soul, not those of the body." Leili Anvar, *Malak Jan Nemati: Life Isn't Short, But Time Is Limited* (New York: Arpeggio Press, 2012), 111.

religions that cater to appearances. Once they have become ensnared, it is unfortunately quite difficult, if not impossible, to convince them of their error, at least in this lifetime.

Essence-Bearers

Essence-bearers are exceptional spiritual personalities who, commensurate with the station and capacity of their soul, bear within them a certain "amount" of His radiating Essence and can in turn transmit His thought, power, will, and light to that same extent. Whether this radiance is as limited as a molecule or as vast as the sea (or greater still), it fulfills the same function for all beings as the Essence Itself. The extent of this radiance in those who bear the Essence determines their power, position, and rank in the spiritual realm. So numerous are the positions and ranks within this hierarchy that they border on the infinite, ultimately culminating in the One. For those who bear the Essence permanently, it has become an integral and permanent part of their being; such individuals never relinquish this Essence, whether in this world or beyond.[2]

At the summit of those who bear the Essence is the *Point of Unicity* (the One in tangible form),[3] who permanently bears the totality of the

---

2. In certain mystical traditions, Essence-bearers are sometimes referred to as "kings." (Ostad Elahi, Commentary on *Haqq ol-Haqāyeq* (*Shāhnāme-ye Haqiqat*), by Hādj Nematollāh Jeyhunābādi [Tehran: Jeyhun, 1994]) If this radiating Essence is provisional within a "king" (whether for an instant or throughout his or her earthly life), that individual is said to "host" the Essence; if the radiance is permanent, he or she is said to be an Essence-bearer. Every human soul bears within it a divine spark that stems from the One, but the "amount" of this spark is insufficient for the soul to be deemed an Essence-bearer. Those who come to know this divine spark come to know themselves and to know God within them (see Fig. 6).

3. For more on the *Point of Unicity*, see the Epilogue. "Those who are engaged in

Essence and can be considered as indistinguishable from the One. A direct throughway—the *metacausal gravitational axis*—always extends from the *Point of Unicity* toward Perfection; negative entities for the human soul dare not approach this axis.

Divine Light (Light of the One)

Divine light, which emanates from the Essence, bears metacausal energy[4] and confers the discernment of Truth. Each time Divine light is reflected upon us—the One directs His attention toward us—in addition to providing metacausal energy, it also inoculates our reason with an "amount" of discernment that proportionally develops our sound reason. The amount of this discernment depends on the level, station, and mission of those who emit this Divine light, as well as the intensity they choose to impart to it.

The discernment of Truth is a capacity that stems from our sound reason and enables us to discern *living real divine truths* from defunct or imaginary divine truths. Once this capacity for the discernment of Truth is developed, it becomes an integral part of our soul's genetic makeup and stays with us permanently, guarding us from all manner of spiritual deception, whether in this world or in the other. As for metacausal

---

their process of spiritual perfection try to first focus their thoughts on the *Point of Unicity*. [Why] the '*Point of Unicity*' and not the 'Source of Unicity'? Because in referring to a 'Source,' what is sought is a generality, whereas in referring to a point the intent is to focus the mind to reach a singularity: the *Point of Unicity*." Ostad Elahi, *Āsār ol-Haqq*, vol. 1, saying 580.

4. The sole source of metacausal energy is the One, but Essence-bearers can also emit metacausal energy commensurate with their spiritual level, rank, and mission. Henceforth, whenever "metacausal energy" is cited in this work, its source should always be understood as the One, regardless of whether such energy emanates directly from the Source, or indirectly through an Essence-bearer.

energy, it renders the soul alive,[5] alert, and active, preventing one from falling into a state of spiritual torpor—the inability to focus on God and to fulfill one's spiritual duties. More importantly, it is the only energy capable of neutralizing the powerful and at the same time spiritually harmful energy of the imperious self.

All of us, in our own culturally distinct way, can direct our attention toward the Source and thus harness Divine light. But the natural way to continuously harness Divine light in an appropriate (physiological) amount is through the practice of *constant attention.* The practice of constant attention does not imply withdrawing from the world, abandoning one's family and society, and retreating to some corner to focus on the supernatural or to engage in repeated formulaic mantras or incantations of God. Rather, having constant attention is much like becoming cognizant of the air that we breath: Just as we become aware of the air that surrounds us upon directing our attention to it, so too can we become aware of the divine flux that surrounds us by directing our attention to it in the normal course of daily life. Hence, we must strive to see this divine flux (imbued with the thought, power, and will of the One) as enveloping us and [in turn] act in accord with the voice of our conscience and divine contentment.

As long as we do not take the initiative to direct our attention— through the divine flux—toward the One (the original God), we should not expect Him to look upon us; He will not do so (save for any exceptions). Indeed, it is incumbent on us (it is our duty) to train ourselves to turn our attention toward Him if we wish for Him to look

---

5. Our soul never perishes, but it can become weak or lazy, or even regress. The soul of one who is disinterested in and utterly disengaged from matters related to God, ethics, or spirituality can be considered "dead."

upon us in turn. Toward that end, all that is needed is to make an effort in our daily activities to act in accord with the voice of our conscience and divine contentment.

Living Real Divine Truths

Living real divine truths are truths that originate from the One or from an authentic God. Together with Divine light and the spiritual provisions we accumulate, these truths (which develop our sound reason) constitute the essential nutrients of our soul.[6] Some of these truths concern theoretical concepts while others pertain to ethical practice.

Living real divine truths relating to theoretical concepts are belief-based axiomatic principles, such as belief in the existence of the One or a true God, the soul, life after death, and especially an accounting.[7] By contrast, *living real divine truths* that pertain to ethical practice are those that entail the application of correct divine and ethical principles.

Indeed, if the axiomatic truths we have embraced in relation to our beliefs are to become palpable, we must first apply the *living real divine truths* that pertain to ethical practice in an *in vivo* manner; there is no other way. The practice of these ethical principles is essentially based upon respecting the legitimate rights of our body, our soul, and others, as well as engaging in beneficence.

---

6. Without nutritional intake, the soul cannot develop and is incapable of undergoing its process of spiritual perfection. Divine light is absorbed by being attentive to God (*constant attention*); *living real divine truths* set forth by *Divine guidance* are assimilated through their *in vivo* practice; and spiritual provisions are acquired through the performance of good deeds, especially altruistic and devotional acts that are carried out selflessly.

7. See chap. 10, "Why Believe in an Accounting?"

In referring to *correct* divine and ethical principles, as well as *living* and *real* divine truths, the choice and sequence of each of these qualifiers is highly relevant:

- "Correct" implies that the divine and ethical principles discussed here have been issued by the Source of Truth and culled, revived, and updated by *Divine guidance*. This condition is imperative if a divine or ethical principle is to nourish the human soul and develop its sound reason.

- "Living" implies that these divine truths are charged with the divine effect (their active ingredient) and are not defunct. A statement of divine truth is defunct when it lacks the divine effect, either because it originates from a source that does not bear the Essence and is unqualified (it has not been designated by the Source), or because it has drifted from its initial meaning due to misguided interpretations. It is thus comparable to medication that lacks its active ingredient or has expired, or to food that lacks any nutritional value or is even downright harmful. Putting into practice such a defunct truth promotes arrogance, pride, superiorism, and garrulousness by feeding our common reason, and if the thoughts of a *venomous individual* lie at its root,[8] it will also have a toxic effect on the soul, poisoning and rendering it dysfunctional.

- "Real" in reference to a divine truth emphasizes that it does not stem from one's imagination, but rather from a source that bears the Essence. By contrast, "imaginary divine truths" are perceived

---

8. For more on venomous individuals, see *Fundamentals*, vol. 4, *Worlds and Interworlds*, chap. 5 (forthcoming).

truths that are in fact false. This is the case, for instance, when a person firmly but mistakenly believes a spiritual guide to be true—to bear the Essence—and faithfully applies his or her prescriptions as real divine truths with the expectation that they will lead him or her to the Truth. Believing in and practicing imaginary divine truths is not only ineffectual for the soul, but may also prove harmful, arresting its progress and even causing it to regress. Note that when the practice of real divine truths is intended as a means of profiteering and deception, it will have a negative effect on the soul.

If we can come to believe these two fundamental truths—(1) that the spiritual world is more vast, vivid, real, alive, active, tangible, and concrete for our soul (our real self) than the material world, and (2) that the same foundational principles (gravitation, opposites, causality, legitimate rights, connection, *in vivo* practice, acceptability, etc.) apply there as they do here in the material world—we can mitigate the spiritual disorientation that has (and continues to) beset humanity, and thus become less susceptible to flawed judgment in matters relating to the meaning of life, spirituality, God, the other world, etc.

By way of illustration, obtaining a medical degree requires that one be accepted (affiliated or connected) to an accredited medical school, study and practice *in vivo* coursework that is up-to-date (living), and successfully pass the corresponding tests (exams) on theory and practice, whereupon one can engage in further research and eventually attain a full professorship. Similarly, to advance through the spiritual levels that culminate in Perfection, we must actively connect ourselves to *Divine guidance*, practice *in vivo* the *living real divine truths* that are presented, and pass the corresponding theoretical and practical tests (trials) until we acquire self-knowledge (our "doctorate"), or knowledge of the divine spark within our soul (Fig. 6); thereafter, we must continue our efforts until we attain a professorship (Perfection). In both cases, we must practice pertinent living real truths, and not defunct or imaginary truths.

The way our theoretical knowledge of spirituality is gauged is no different than the way our theoretical knowledge of any experimental science is gauged. Our spiritual practice, on the other hand, is assessed on the basis of our *in vivo* reactions to the imperious self. What is our reaction, for instance, when our feelings of jealousy or greed are provoked? Do we respond positively—i.e., refrain from acting on our jealousy and suppress our greed—in which case we would pass our test and take a step forward in our process of spiritual perfection? Or do we respond negatively—i.e., follow through on our feelings of jealousy and greed—and thus fail our test? These tests recur throughout our life (or future lives) as often as necessary until we ultimately succeed in passing them—i.e., gaining mastery over our feelings of jealousy or greed. It is also possible that we may not succeed in passing these tests.

The same process applies to all our other character weak points as well, such as pride and arrogance, irascibleness, vengefulness, and lustfulness. There are some who fail on the very first test that wounds their pride, leading them at times to haughtily turn away from God and spirituality, as if they had hitherto been doing God a favor by believing in Him. As a general rule, we must continue to fight against the imperious self—which is generated from the activity of our character weak points and flaws relating to divine or ethical principles—until we can come to control and master our character weak points.

Character Weak Points and the Imperious Self

"The tests that a student of spirituality [of the new medicine of the soul] is confronted with are always based on his or her weak points."[9] The switch that activates our weak points is triggered either from within (by our own thoughts) or from without (e.g., by other people); hence, we must be attentive to whom we socialize with. An example of this activation is the decision, under pressure from the imperious self, to pursue someone or to possess something without any regard for issues of consent.

The imperious self is produced by the activity of one's character weak points and flaws relating to divine or ethical principles. At the level of the conscious self, it constantly manifests as a flux of emotional or argumentative thoughts that stands in opposition to correct divine and ethical principles. Within our conscious self, each of us experiences the imperious self as impulses, desires, or thoughts (temptations) that are contrary to divine and ethical principles and pleasing to our ego, pressuring our psyche to indulge them.

The pleasure derived from the imperious self always runs counter to correct divine and ethical principles. The initial spark that inflames the imperious self can differ among men and women. For men, it mostly stems from libido and the will to power, while in women it mostly stems from sentiments of jealousy, the desire for revenge, and the exaggerated need for attention.

It is important to note that evil is not created by God, but rather results from the imperious self of human beings. The minds of most people are dominated by their imperious self, with the exception of those who are self-aware and who actively seek to fight their imperious self.

9. Ostad Elahi, *Āsār ol-Haqq*, vol. 2, saying 50.

In every era, real divine truths are culled, revived, and updated by *Divine guidance*. "Culled" means that these real divine truths are extracted from the mass of imaginary or defunct divine truths among which they are buried; "revived" signifies that these truths are recharged with their divine effect; and "updated" indicates that they are adapted to the evolution of human thought, such that they can be understood and applied by the people of that era.

Just as the essential nature and functioning of the soul is uniform for all human beings throughout time—for example, by nature all humans endowed with reason have an imperious self and an inner guide[10]—the divine truths originally issued by the Source of Truth for the education and development of the human soul fundamentally remain the same; only the manner in which they are expressed and the modalities of their application change over time. In each era, these truths are presented and made available to everyone by *Divine guidance*; they are not bound by geography or culture, nor are they under the province of any one person or group.

It remains up to us to actively seek these truths and connect to *Divine guidance* by way of our thought or, better yet, with the added benefit of physical interaction if possible. Connecting by means of one's thought alone is similar to learning by correspondence, whereas the added element of physical interaction makes the process more akin to in-person learning, the standard method of instruction in the experimental sciences.

Authentic *Divine guidance*—in the sense that it is directly connected to the Source of Truth (the One)—mirrors the attributes of the One. Such guidance has no need for recognition or publicity. Likewise, the

---

10. See chap. 9.

designated representative who is truly entrusted with *Divine guidance* in each era by the One—no matter how high the rank of his or her Essence—tends toward a normal and discrete life, remaining active in society while earning a livelihood like his or her peers.[11]

Representatives entrusted with *Divine guidance* avoid any form of bluster or self-promotion regarding their spiritual status and do not flaunt their spiritual power, no matter how great. Upright and honest, they loathe hypocrisy and duplicity. Regardless of whether it is pleasing to people's egos, they present the Truth as it is, in a poised and rational manner, without resorting to polemics or invoking their spiritual power to impose their words upon others.

All human beings who *sincerely seek the Truth*, no matter where they are or what beliefs they hold, will be connected—by way of their thought—to *Divine guidance* by the Creator and guided toward the Source of Truth, whether they are conscious of it or not. In these instances, the Source will inspire them to act correctly, which in turn will naturally draw them toward the Truth. The essential requisite is to sincerely seek the Truth. According to the principle of connection, the Creator will not allow those who are sincere in their pursuit of the Truth to become

---

11. Spirituality must never be monetized under any circumstance, much less serve as a source of one's livelihood. Thus, those who have a direct connection to the Source ensure their own livelihood and that of their family through their own work, so that they are not dependent on anyone and are able to speak the Truth, even if it is not to the liking of others' egos. Speaking the Truth always runs counter to illegitimate and unethical pleasures, which are among the most attractive for the ego. Those who are financially dependent on others, if only for a pittance, cannot always speak the Truth; they are obligated to say that which pleases the ego of others, even if it is contrary to the Truth.

disoriented or to fall prey either to deceivers or the deceived;[12] ultimately, He will connect them to *Divine guidance* by way of their thought.

In summary, inasmuch as *living real divine truths* bear the divine effect, they develop our sound reason. By contrast, defunct or imaginary divine truths lack the divine effect and thus solely feed our common reason, promoting philosophical sophistry and rhetoric in our minds, while heightening superstition, worship of falsities,[13] and futile pursuits. As for venomous principles, they poison the soul. It is for this reason that those who are engaged in a religion, spiritual path, or philosophical school of thought are advised to exercise caution. To avoid any harm to their souls, they should ask themselves: (1) What is their goal in seeking spirituality? (2) What principles (theoretical and practical) are being conveyed to them, and from what source do they originate? And (3) Who is being introduced as a role model? Does, or did, this person bear the Essence?

---

12. Spiritually deceived individuals are those who sincerely believe in and earnestly promote a false religion or misguided spiritual path.

13. Worship of a falsity refers to worshiping that which stands in opposition to a *real* Truth. For example, instead of worshipping God, one is drawn to worship its opposite.

Chapter 4

The Quintessence of Religions

Today, the multiplicity of beliefs in a contentious marketplace for influence and the spread of numerous spiritual, religious, and philosophical paths have made it increasingly difficult to distinguish truth from falsity and to discern divine principles that are *real* from those that are *imaginary* and, in particular, toxic. Within such a context, Ostad's words in "The Quintessence of Religions"[1] may offer some clarity and guidance:

1) Place your faith in the unique God and rely only on Him in the depths of your heart. Consider Him as the Efficient in all matters; the rest are but the means and machinery of causality.

2) Consider all beings as good, for He does not create evil. If a person commits an evil act, it is the act that is "evil"; your duty is to strive to eschew such evil in all its forms. With regard to those who are considered good,[2] respect them and their legacy[3] in the custom and manner by which they have come to be known.

---

1. Ostad Elahi, *Borhān ol-Haqq*, 8th ed. (Tehran: Jeyhun, 1994), 306.
2. Such individuals include authentic prophets and saints of the past, as well as the benefactors of humanity (philanthropists, inventors that have benefited humankind, etc.) in every time and place.
3. One should respect, for example, sacred texts such as the Avesta, the Torah, the Gospels, the Quran, or the sayings attributed to the Buddha, regardless of one's views as to their historical authenticity or accuracy.

On Evil and Satan

"Satan is none other than the projections, manipulations, and choices of the malicious and impulsive imperious self of arrogant ungodly individuals."[4]

Evil originates from the imperious self of human beings. Part of our essential human duty is to fight against our imperious self in order to cultivate our altruistic and human dimension, thereby contributing to reducing "evil" in society and serving as an example to others. Legend has it that when Nimrod, king of Chaldea, commanded Abraham to worship him as the only God, Abraham replied: "There is only one God worthy of worship. You are not God; the Creator alone can be known as such—it is for Him to grant or take life." Nimrod declared: "I too have the power to grant or take your life." He then ordered a large pyre to be built and had Abraham thrown into it from the top of a tower. A bee was seen scurrying between the pyre and a stream, trickling drops of water over the pyre with each passage. When it was told that its drops would amount to nothing, it responded, "Indeed, but in the face of evil, God expects of us only that of which we are capable."

3) In every time and in every place, abide by and advocate that which the wise in society deem good and righteous—that is, the laws and regulations based on a system of rights and meritocracy that enable all individuals to claim their legitimate due, thereby ensuring social order and peace—and avoid all that is to the contrary.

4) Beyond that, any creed[5] you choose is acceptable, provided

---

4. Ostad Elahi, *Borhān ol-Haqq*, 340.

5. All authentic religions at their origin are based on unicity. Their goal is to

that it does not conflict with these stated principles and you faithfully put its precepts into practice.

One can summarize Ostad's "Quintessence of Religions" as such: to have faith in the One or in a true God;[6] to fight against our imperious self, which is the source of evil within each of us; to respect legitimate rights, including our own rights and those of others and society (civil laws); and to practice beneficence. The application of these principles lessens our selfishness and biological propensity to infringe on the rights of others, gradually elevating us to a greater state of compassion and humanity. In short, we are transformed into a true human being.[7]

Why Practice Ethics?

It is through the *in vivo* practice of correct ethical principles that we can cultivate our humanity. Ethics in its purest form is based on the observance of rights—in particular the rights of others—and the practice of beneficence. These rights encompass one's own legitimate rights—including those of our soul and our body-id[8]—and especially the legitimate rights of others (i.e., our fellow beings, animals, nature, society, etc.).

The pure animal nature of human beings (the id) is similar to that of other primates, but the addition of reason alters its pure state and

---

cultivate faith in the unique God and to encourage the observance of rights—especially those of others—and the practice of beneficence.

6. Those who believe in the God of one of the authentic monotheistic religions believe in a true God.

7. The measure by which one can distinguish a true human being (*ensān*) from a human-animal (*bashar*) is that the former strives to think and act in accordance with the voice of his or her conscience, whereas the latter acts in accordance with the desires of his or her selfish ego.

8. The body-id refers to our physical body and our pure animal nature.

renders its attributes bidimensional instead (i.e., capable of tending toward good or evil). If these attributes become aberrant, they will transform into character weak points and flaws relating to divine or ethical principles, and it is the activity of these weak points in turn that leads to the formation of the imperious self.

If we wish to cultivate our humanity, it is imperative that we engage in the *in vivo* practice of ethics in every circumstance, whether we are by ourselves or in the presence of others. It is only possible to observe ethics in every circumstance if we set Perfection as our goal (Perfection that is realized by first coming to know oneself and then by coming to know God); otherwise, given that the human psyche is constantly in flux, we may at times not observe ethics, and even go so far as to arrogate the right to commit unethical acts. We humans are such that in the absence of constraints rooted in ethics and belief in the Divine, we inevitably transform into cruel, transgressive, and scheming predators that bring ruin upon ourselves and others in society.

Chapter 5

Divine Guidance

Divine guidance is always present on earth, but it falls upon us to diligently and persistently seek and connect ourselves to it.

In order to know which direction to pursue in spirituality, we must strive to connect ourselves to *Divine guidance*. As long as we are in this world, this guidance points us toward true spirituality and sets forth that which we should espouse and act upon, and that which we should disregard and dismiss. In addition, it will help us to know our imperious self—the origin of all evil and the root cause of misguidance—and show us how to effectively fight against it.

Divine guidance is always present on all planets that have beings endowed with reason, including earth. This guidance can be considered as the *metacausal gravitational axis* that directly links the ecosystem of spiritual life on earth to the Source of Truth, and is under the aegis of the *Point of Unicity*.[1] Along this axis, the exertion of metacausal gravitation on the soul and psyche is substantial. Those who are able to establish and sincerely maintain a connection to this axis throughout their entire life

---

1. The *Point of Unicity* is the One in tangible form that permanently bears the totality of the Essence (see Epilogue). It is not necessary to know the identity of the *Point of Unicity*; it suffices to know only that the *Point of Unicity* exists. All of us, whatever our faith or creed, can seek His help and guidance by means of our thought.

can be hopeful to eventually reach their ultimate goal. Spiritual entities deemed negative for the human soul dare not approach this axis. Hence, those who succeed here in sincerely connecting themselves to this axis can continue to advance toward their goal, without losing their way or being misled by negative entities (which are always lying in wait for those who are engaged in a spiritual path).

Without either a direct or indirect connection to *Divine guidance*, it is all but certain that we will spiritually stray, and none can reach the ultimate goal. Indeed, in the absence of this connection, we cannot know which spiritual goal, beliefs, or practices to adopt or to dismiss. Moreover, we will fail to recognize our need for metacausal energy, without which it is impossible to withstand, much less neutralize, the constant pressure of the recurring impulses and desires of our imperious self. As such, we must diligently seek—and this is part of our essential duty—to connect our thought to *Divine guidance.* Toward this end, and to prepare ourselves to sincerely seek the Truth (the One) and the *living real divine truths* set forth by *Divine guidance,* we must impress upon ourselves that our soul (which never dies) constitutes our real self, and that our life continues in the other world (the spiritual worlds). In principle, the Creator will connect to *Divine guidance* all those who sincerely (from their heart) seek the Truth, regardless of their beliefs or culture; if this connection is not accessible physically, He will guide them through their own thoughts and the voice of their conscience.

Once we have come to recognize—by way of *Divine guidance*—our ultimate goal, and have come to know the beliefs and practices we ought to espouse or reject, we will be able to more regularly control, and more frequently neutralize, the assaults of our imperious self with the help of our inner guide and support from the metacausal energy of the One (which is harnessed through the divine flux).

Divine guidance is marked by the following characteristics:

(1) It helps us to understand that the sense of self within us stems from our soul.

(2) It cultivates *true monotheism* within us. A true monotheist is one who has sincere faith in a true God (such as the God of one of the authentic monotheistic religions) and knows that "God" is but One. All authentic historical Gods are merged into the One (the original God). It is we humans who have created a distinction in our minds by attributing many names to Him. All sincere believers, provided they have placed their faith in a true God, are connected to the One and in fact worship the same God, the One. Moreover, there are some individuals in society who abide by the voice of their conscience, sincerely practice ethics, and are beneficent toward others, and yet cannot come to accept God as presented by today's religions. The One will not let such individuals completely stagnate in their process of spiritual perfection, and will eventually bring them to know the true God, be it during their life on earth or in the interworld. For what is the voice of conscience but the echo of the voice of God within us? Those who truly act in accord with the voice of their conscience are in effect in contact with God.

(3) It sets forth a method for the sound development of one's thought, whose curriculum is based on *living real divine truths*. The sole objective of this sound development of thought is to lead us toward self-knowledge (knowledge of the divine spark

within our soul; Fig. 6) and, from there, to Perfection. The sound development of one's thought is implemented through the practice of *natural spirituality*. This spirituality is referred to as "natural" because it requires that we strive to always (a) take into account the legitimate natural rights of the soul as well as those of the body-id, and (b) maintain a regular state of self-consciousness while avoiding altered states that impair our reason. In addition, we should refrain from physically harsh ascetic practices, all manner of bizarre behaviors, and empty fanciful utterances.

(4) It helps us to understand that upon death, the self leaves our physical body and continues to the interworld in the form of a *subtle body*, a more delicate, weightless, and transparent version of our physical body. The length of our stay(s) in the interworld can vary in duration.

(5) It encourages us to pay attention to an "accounting" in the hereafter; that is, to be aware that our actions and thoughts during our life on earth are fully, accurately, and contemporaneously recorded within the depths of our being (our soul) and will serve as the basis for one's evaluation once we are in the hereafter. Furthermore, it makes us aware (based on the principle of causality) that we will not obtain anything in the hereafter without first doing something of positive value for our true self while living here on earth.

(6) It does not impose any principle or prescription on anyone. It simply sets forth the curriculum for the sound development of one's thought (*living real divine truths*) and encourages those

who wish to grasp (from the depths of their being) the beneficial effects of these truths to apply them *in vivo* and not to merely settle for an *in vitro* (theoretical) approach.

(7) It teaches us that as long as we are living here on earth, we have but one essential duty that takes precedence over all our other duties—namely, to complete the fundamental stage in our process of spiritual perfection (which can only be done here on earth), while at the same time leading an active social and family life. What is intended by "duty" here is that the responsibility for undertaking the process of spiritual perfection (our essential duty) falls upon us: no one will compel us, and any compulsion must be self-imposed.

(8) It teaches us how to develop *constant attention* within and to transform it into *perfect attention*. Constant attention is to have our attention directed toward God and to consider Him present and observant by way of the divine flux, whereas perfect attention is to have our attention simultaneously directed toward God and the activities of our imperious self. Perfect attention enables us to continuously harness the metacausal energy of the One in a physiological dose that is adapted to the nature of our soul and psyche, while at the same time allowing us to constantly monitor the ever-harmful activities of our imperious self.[2]

(9) It teaches us what the imperious self is, how to identify it within

---

2. Within each person endowed with reason and discernment is produced a negative energy that is harmful to the soul. This psychological energy exists in a potential state and can be activated by an internal or external stimulus. When this energy becomes active and surfaces at the level of our conscious self, one speaks of the "imperious self" or the "activity of the imperious self."

us, and how to prevent and fight against it until it is neutralized. It encourages us to prioritize in our spiritual work the *in vivo* practice of correct divine and ethical principles, including beneficence and the observance of legitimate rights, with an emphasis on those of our fellow beings. Indeed, knowingly and intentionally transgressing the legitimate rights of another solely for the satisfaction of our own ego is considered a grave misdeed, one that we will have to answer for, unless the victim himself or herself (the holder of that right) were to forgive us. In the other world, obtaining a victim's forgiveness is difficult, if not at times impossible, unless God were to come to our aid (i.e., by making the victim whole such that he or she assents to our forgiveness). But for God to intervene in this manner, we must have acquired the merit for it during our life on earth.

(10) It fosters within us the principle—which regrettably is increasingly neglected—that without His will, nothing can be done or undone. It teaches us to reiterate this principle within us until our experience confirms that without His will, no one can advance even a single step in the process of spiritual perfection. When we come to think in this manner, both our material and spiritual lives will become more manageable and our minds will be more at ease.

(11) It encourages us to lead an active life in society, diligently avoiding retreating from the world or living a parasitic existence in any shape or form. It also encourages us to advance our education to the highest level if circumstances allow, and if not, to learn a useful trade in order to manage our own livelihood.

The objective here is for one to be able to earn a dignified living through one's own work, such that one does not have to be reliant on others. If one becomes dependent on others, if only for a pittance, one will not be able to freely pursue the Truth, speak the Truth, or practice the Truth.

(12) It allows us to understand that in the process of spiritual perfection, the teaching of spirituality can in no way constitute a means of earning a livelihood, even if it is only done as a way to secure one's daily bread.[3] Those who live at the expense of their followers should know that the monetary compensation they receive in exchange for their teachings is contrary to the dignity of their soul and will have an extremely adverse effect upon it.

---

3. An exception applies to those whose disability truly prevents them from earning their own livelihood, in which case they should seek only that which is necessary to fulfill their basic needs.

Chapter 6

In Vitro Practice and *In Vivo* Practice

*As long as one does not practice a divine truth
in vivo, its true meaning cannot be grasped.*

In vitro and *in vivo* are commonly applied terms in medicine. *In vitro* often refers to research conducted on a laboratory sample in an experimental setting, whereas *in vivo* refers to research carried out on a living organism. *In vitro* work generally constitutes the preparatory phase that precedes *in vivo* experimentation; as long as a therapeutic hypothesis has not been tested and confirmed in an *in vivo* setting, it cannot be deemed scientifically validated.

These two terms are frequently used in relation to the process of spiritual perfection. *In vitro* practice involves theoretically learning and memorizing a real divine truth, and then reflecting upon and persuading oneself of that truth in preparation for its *in vivo* application. Following this mental preparation, *in vivo* practice entails personally applying this divine truth within the concrete reality of daily life and in our interaction with others. Thus, the complete practice of *living real divine truths* consists of two phases: a preparatory mental phase (memorization, reflection, and self-persuasion), which is carried out *in vitro*, and a practical phase (within real-life situations), which is carried out *in vivo*.

The following example taken from one of Ostad's sayings illustrates the complementary nature of *in vitro* and *in vivo* practice:

When I was in Lār,[1] there was a young man who had lost his father as a child. His paternal aunt, who had been appointed his guardian and had assumed full control of his finances, refused to relinquish control of her nephew's inheritance when he came of age. The aunt had no children of her own and refused to compromise, leading the young man to file a complaint. In accordance with the law, I terminated her guardianship and restored his inheritance to him.

Some time passed after this incident. I had arranged for some judicial attire that required a pair of patent leather shoes. It so happened that the same young man was available, and I gave him money to purchase the shoes for me from Shiraz. During his trip, he ran out of money and spent all the money I had given him. After investigating further, I learned that he had bought the shoes, but then resold them. Upon his return, when I inquired about the shoes, he defensively replied: "I suppose you're going to use your power now and throw me in jail!" I simply told him to leave.

A few days later, this same young man was brought into court for having slapped a respected merchant in public. Given that he had been planning on enlisting in the gendarmerie, his conviction would result in a criminal record that would have precluded his government employment. The merchant was adamant in moving forward with his complaint. I could have sentenced the young man from eight days to two months in jail.

I thus became embroiled in an inner conflict, for at times the desire for revenge can overcome one's heart. I kept fighting my imperious self, telling myself that I should not use my position

---

1. From 1934 to 1937, Ostad served as Justice of the Peace in *Lār*, located in the rural province of *Lārestān*. It was his first post after graduating from the National School of Jurisprudence.

and authority to exact revenge. With considerable struggle, I was finally able to overcome my ego. Knowing that one's words assume a certain effect once the ego has been subdued, I turned to the merchant and said: "No matter how much I have insisted so far, you have refused to forgive this young man, but this decision will impact his future. Now, I appeal to your sense of chivalry and ask whether you can bring yourself to forgive this young man for my sake?" The merchant paused for a moment and agreed to forgive him. I dismissed the young man. Feeling ashamed, he wanted to come and apologize to me. "It's fine," I said, "just let it be." Had I sentenced him to jail, I would have always thought to myself: "See, you did exact your revenge after all."[2]

This example illustrates how after a period of *in vitro* reflection, Ostad reaches a firm decision to overcome his desire for revenge. He then applies the *in vivo* method to practically fight against his impulse for revenge by insisting that the merchant forgive the young man, even though doing so was perceived to be belittling for a judge according to the judicial customs of the time.

---

2. Ostad Elahi, *Āsār ol-Haqq*, vol. 1, saying 1626.

Chapter 7

The Pragmatist and the Idealist

Truth is realized through practice, not words.[1]

T he psyche or *overall mental space* of all human beings is formed by the combination of two spaces with different yet complementary tendencies: the *pragmatic space* and the *idealistic space*.

As a newborn, one naturally possesses the outlines of these two mental spaces, each of which gradually develops throughout one's life under the influence of one's environment, education, and experience. The pragmatic space mostly develops by confronting the concrete realities of life, whereas the idealistic space mostly develops under the influence of one's imagination and imaginings.

The idealistic space complements the pragmatic space and is as necessary and useful as the latter, although it requires that one know how to properly benefit from it. Indeed, emotion and faith manifest and develop within our idealistic mental space, while reason and pragmatism manifest and develop within our pragmatic mental space.

These two spaces behave much like communicating vessels: as one develops and expands, the other diminishes. The dominance of one mental space over the other determines one's psychological temperament.

---

1. Ostad Elahi, *Āsār ol-Haqq*, vol. 1, saying 1152.

If the pragmatic mental space is dominant, one will tend to be pragmatic and realistic; if the idealistic mental space is dominant, one will tend to be idealistic and prone to reverie. In general, the psyche (our overall mental space), which is the ensemble formed by these two spaces, is marked by plasticity and is quite malleable; through the use of our willpower, it can be molded like wax into any form that we wish. For example, with the help of strong willpower, idealistic persons prone to reverie can gradually transform into pragmatic and realistic individuals.

Unless compelled otherwise, idealistic individuals by nature tend to avoid confronting the concrete realities of life *in vivo*, preferring instead to manage the problems of daily life *in vitro*, i.e., at a mental level. Take, for instance, an idealistic person who decides to develop the virtue of forgiveness until that virtue becomes second nature. Imagine that such a person were wronged by another out of jealousy. In an attempt to replace his rancor with forgiveness, the idealist habitually enters his overall mental space and repeatedly engages in autosuggestion (an *in vitro* method) until he mentally forgives that person and even contentedly comes to believe that he has truly done so; he no longer deems it necessary to challenge himself in an *in vivo* manner (in direct contact with that person) to practically determine whether he has truly forgiven that person or only imagined having done so. An individual who has thus solely relied on an *in vitro* approach will find that when he subsequently encounters that same person in real life, his forgiveness was in fact imaginary and that his rancor and dislike of that person remain. This is due to the fact that he has not complemented his *in vitro* practice with an *in vivo* one.

Or, suppose that this same person, having suffered from being spoken ill of behind his back, develops a strong aversion toward backbiting and decides to rid himself of this ethical weak point or flaw, which is found in nearly everyone. He spontaneously engages in an *in vitro* practice within his overall mental space until he convinces himself he has overcome his tendency to backbite and feels content with his effort. Yet, when he finds himself confronted with the concrete reality of life—that is, when he is once again among friends or colleagues with whom he would habitually engage in backbiting—he realizes that in practice he is unable to resist joining them in speaking ill of others.

Now, consider a pragmatic person who wants to fight against one of her character weak points, such as exclusionary selfishness (a weakness that drives one to want everything good solely for oneself, without taking into account that others also have rights). She begins by delving within her psyche (overall mental space) and engaging in self-reasoning (an *in vitro* practice) about the harms of exclusionary selfishness, until she makes a firm decision to tame[2] this weak point and turn it into altruism. Subsequently, because her pragmatic nature directs her toward an *in vivo* practice rooted in concrete reality, she spontaneously chooses to interact with others and forces herself to behave altruistically, which requires a degree of selflessness (the opposite of selfishness). She begins this practice in relation to those who are close[3] to her and her acquaintances before extending it to others, until by dint of repetition the virtues of altruism and selflessness gradually replace her selfishness. Encouraged by the resultant well-being and serenity that she feels, she applies this same *in vivo* practice to her other character weak points or flaws (relating

---

2. As our character weak points are dominated by various animal traits within us, the word "tame" is deliberately used here in relation to controlling them.
3. For those who live as a couple, it is recommended that they begin this practice with their partner or spouse; others can begin with their family members, for example.

to divine or ethical principles) until she is able, through repetition, to master them as well.

Given that our psyche (overall mental space) is a combination of two mental spaces (pragmatic and idealistic), even pragmatists have a more or less idealistic and fanciful side, but their pragmatic mental space is more developed and active, whereas in idealists it is their idealistic or imaginary mental space that dominates. In reality, all human beings have a tendency to initially evaluate a situation in their psyche (overall mental space), but when it comes time to act, some adopt a pragmatic approach and others an idealistic one. Moreover, when their material interests are at stake, most people strive to be pragmatic to avoid any potential loss, yet when it comes to ethics or spirituality, they tend to behave as idealists.

There are also some idealistic individuals who, by reason of their sincere faith in *Divine guidance* and their enthusiasm for the pursuit of spiritual perfection, diligently learn and commit to memory the *living real divine truths* taught by such guidance, instilling and reiterating them in their minds. Although they naturally tend toward an *in vitro* practice and are disinclined to engage in an *in vivo* practice, the truths they memorize with complete faith and reiterate to themselves will nonetheless be extremely beneficial, advancing them in their process of perfection and in some ways preparing their souls. When such individuals return to the interworld, higher levels will be accessible to them and they will benefit from a greater familiarity with their surroundings, for we all appear in the hereafter with the same "mental baggage" that we carry here in this world. Thus, it is highly likely that they will acquire the acceptability to be kept there and not sent back to earth, to this world of spiritual amnesia, with its painful constraints and incessant conflicts. In the interworld, they will more readily understand and apply the spiritual teachings they receive, and will advance more rapidly than those who did not receive a spiritual education during their stay on earth.

In summary, pragmatists, after first analyzing matters in their overall mental space (an *in vitro* practice), have a natural tendency to act in an *in vivo* manner—i.e., to act within the concrete reality of life—until they can come to grasp the deeper meaning behind the truth of each matter. By contrast, idealists are content with an *in vitro* practice, for they believe that the deeper meaning of truths can be grasped through words. Yet words alone are incapable of allowing one to grasp the deeper meaning of the ideas they convey. For example, as long as we have not tasted a certain food, we cannot know its flavor; by analogy, as long as we have not put into practice *in vivo* that which we have understood through words, we will not be able to grasp its truth. Simply put, both idealists and pragmatists derive meaning from the words they reflect upon, as if they were figuratively preparing a "cognitive meal" for their psyche. But whereas pragmatists consume the meal, idealists content themselves with simply observing it or savoring its aroma.

Furthermore, given that idealists do not interact with concrete realities, the taste of failure is less familiar to them. They thus become prone to a sense of pride and arrogance,[4] which is the foremost obstacle to one's process of spiritual perfection. Should such idealists choose to engage in spirituality, they will automatically develop a form of *spiritual superioritism*, a state that may prevent them from concretely advancing toward their spiritual perfection: It would be as though they were seated behind the steering wheel of their soul, with a full tank of gas

---

4. See Ostad Elahi, *Paroles de Vérité*, saying 338.

and the engine running, but attempted to accelerate in neutral instead.[5] Conversely, insofar as pragmatists engage in the concrete practice of spirituality, they know full well the taste of failure and are more cognizant of their weaknesses, which inevitably makes them more humble and less arrogant.

Divine light and *living real divine truths* are among the essential nutrients for the development of the human soul. These two nutrients are complementary: they develop our sound reason and, in parallel, our soul. In principle, each time that we focus our attention on Him, we come to absorb Divine light. As for *living real divine truths*, they must be practiced *in vivo* if they are to be assimilated by the soul, a prerequisite for developing and transforming the latter into the Truth; *in vitro* practice alone will not suffice. "Transforming into the Truth" implies aligning and strengthening the gravitational affinity of one's soul in relation to that of the Source of Truth (the One), such that the soul can come to be accepted by the exalted spiritual "heavens."

We should therefore strive to be pragmatic in our spiritual practice: We must first engage in an *in vitro* analysis of each *living real divine truth* and impress it upon ourselves. We must subsequently implement that truth *in vivo* to obtain tangible results. If we do not practice *living real divine truths in vivo*, we will merely accumulate some theoretical information in the archives of our memory, which, though not entirely devoid of value, remains wholly insufficient. "Truth is realized through practice, not words."[6]

------

5. See chap. 17.
6. See note 1.

Chapter 8

Our Real Self
Commentary on Figure 1

O ur real self is our soul. At the level of our conscious self, the soul manifests as the sense of self. Each time the topic of the human soul is raised in this *Guide*, it refers to the *human soul proper*, a bidimensional soul that results from the combination of a human celestial soul (bearing "angelic," celestial characteristics) and a terrestrial soul specific to the human embryo (bearing terrestrial, purely animal characteristics). Without the celestial dimension of the human soul present in the physical body, we humans would merely be humanoid primates, having neither reason nor a moral conscience, faith, willpower . . .

Thoughts and decisions are formed within the soul before manifesting in the brain and psyche.[1] For example, when I say that "I" am going to do, or not do, something, this "I" stems from my soul. It is my soul (my real self) that induces my brain and psyche to engage, or not engage, in something; my brain and psyche simply execute the soul's commands. That is why once we are in the hereafter, it is our soul (our real self)

---

1. Our thoughts and decisions manifest in the brain and psyche, much like a lamp illuminates a dark room. For example, the source of electricity for a flashlight is its battery, but it is in its bulb that this electric source manifests as light. "The source and seat of our emotions (attractions, repulsions, etc.) and feelings lies in the heart [the soul], and the brain is but an instrument for the heart." Ostad Elahi, *Āsār ol-Haqq*, vol. 1, saying 308.

that will be held to account and not the physical body that we have left behind.

Contrary to what is commonly believed, the human psyche is not the equivalent of the soul, but rather only a component of it. As long as the human soul is present in its physical body,[2] however, the principle of causality requires that it interact with its worldly environment through the brain and psyche.

Fig. 1a – Body or Soul: Which Is Our Real Self?

Our real self is our soul. The physical body is like a provisional matrix (womb) that enables the soul to interact with its worldly environment—through the brain and psyche—in order to nourish itself and develop. In the material world, the soul and the body are mutually necessary. As such, the physical body is not capable of sustaining the process of life without the soul, just as the latter cannot engage in its process of perfection without the contributions of the former (via the psyche).

Every being has a "soul" that endows it with a consciousness and comprehension specific to its own nature. The more evolved a being in its process of perfection, the more developed its soul and the higher its capacity for consciousness. For example, earthly minerals are endowed

---

2. Human celestial souls have their own specific celestial "Origin"; regardless of where they may be, their connection to this "Origin" is never severed. The relationship of a human celestial soul to the human body amounts to a form of radiance: this radiance translates into a *functional* presence within the body, as if the soul actually resided within it. (See Ostad Elahi, *Paroles de Vérité*, saying 376.) As soon as the soul leaves the physical body—i.e., it ceases to radiate within the body—the body truly dies and no force can subsequently restore that soul to its body and revive it to its prior state, unless by divine command (in accordance with the principle of exception).

with the most basic form of consciousness, whereas humans, by virtue of their reason, are endowed with the highest capacity for consciousness and comprehension.

Fig. 1b – Representation of the Human Soul Proper and Its Psyche

In this figure, the human soul is depicted as a large bubble, and the psyche—which is but one of its components—is depicted as a smaller bubble in the *terrestrial pole* of the soul.

The totality of the human soul is consciousness, a consciousness that bears reason, a moral conscience, faith, willpower . . . Yet, as long as the soul is present in the body, an opaque veil of thought—the *psychological veil*—divides and separates this consciousness into two unequal parts. The much smaller part, our *conscious self*, is situated in the conscious realm and concerns itself with the material world. The substantially larger and nearly-total part of our consciousness, our *total unconscious*, is situated in the unconscious realm (like a submerged iceberg) and concerns itself with the spiritual worlds; it is responsible for our direct communication with the spiritual realm. Thus, the concern and focus of our conscious self is mainly life on earth, whereas the concern and focus of our total unconscious is life in the other world.

Souls are of varying groups, set apart by their nature and specificity, varied capacity for consciousness, and innate aptitude. The advantage of the celestial soul specific to humans lies in being innately endowed with specific aptitudes, especially a celestial intelligence of great capacity.[3] If

---

3. The soul's capacity is indicative of its aptitude; thus, the greater a soul's capacity, the greater its aptitude.

actualized, this intelligence enables one to rise to the highest and noblest ranks among creation. But for this to occur, the celestial soul must first become complete—that is, it must become bidimensional. The *human soul proper* results from the combination of a celestial soul specific to humans (which originates directly from God) and a terrestrial soul (the soul of a human embryo and the culminating flux of earth's *vital essence*).

The terrestrial soul, which manifests in the psyche as the *id* (the worker self),[4] has a pure animal nature and instinctively ensures the survival of our physical body. This soul, which is individuated, is just one degree more evolved relative to the soul of higher-order animals (such as primates) that have yet to undergo individuation. The human terrestrial soul contains within it the quintessential properties of the animal souls that have contributed to its formation. This soul (the id) expresses itself at the level of our conscious self in the form of instincts that we share in common with primates and that correspond to our terrestrial-animal needs (hunger and sleep, the sexual instinct and the instinct of reproduction, fear and flight, anger and territoriality, etc.). It is for this reason that one can observe the expression of animal traits in humans as well.

At its inception, the human celestial soul is unidimensional and imperceptible. But when it first merges with a newborn—at the moment of birth and with its first breath—the terrestrial soul's quintessential animal properties dissolve within it and the human celestial soul thereby becomes complete (or bidimensional). Upon becoming bidimensional, it assumes a *psychical state* and transforms into a *human soul proper* (Fig. 4b). Thereafter, a *sense of self,* along with reason and selfish egoity (preferring

---

4. For more on the id, see chap. 11.

for oneself all that one deems good), appears within the human soul proper and it becomes capable of assuming a *subtle body* and rendering itself perceptible. The first physical body and its earthly environment together constitute the human soul's first *body-milieu*.

To undertake its process of perfection, the human soul requires multiple successive lives in this earthly world.[5] With every new body (new body-milieu), the human soul is endowed—in accordance with the *seven creational factors*[6]—with a new brain, psyche, and earthly environment that allow its psyche to acquire new knowledge, both positive and negative. Yet the sense of self that appears within it the first time that the human celestial soul combines with the terrestrial soul of a newborn becomes its permanent identity: This initial sense of self never disappears and is engraved within the human soul, forever accompanying it, whether in this world or in the hereafter. Thus, it is this same "self" that always accompanies us during the course of our successive lives as we go back and forth between this earthly world and the interworld. Upon reaching Perfection, our selfish egoity disappears from our soul, giving way to a generous and empathetic self. In such a state, we become like a "photon" of Divine light.

---

5. According to the principle of ascending successive lives, from its first appearance on earth, every human celestial soul must undertake several lives in a human body to have sufficient time to complete, at a minimum, the fundamental stage of its process of spiritual perfection (see Ostad Elahi, *Ma'refat ol-Ruh*, chap. 7). Once it has completed this fundamental stage, it will obtain the right (the acceptability) to remain in the interworld of planet Earth—where conditions for learning divine truths are far better than they are in this world—to possibly complete the advanced stage in its process of spiritual perfection in order to reach Perfection.

6. See Ostad Elahi, *Borhān ol-Haqq*, 334.

Dignity

Dignity is a quality that stems from the human celestial soul and is cultivated through the assimilation of correct divine and ethical principles. To become dignified is to cultivate within one's psyche correct divine and ethical principles until they have become second nature and to adopt a comportment reflective of a true human being. Those who truly sense the dignity of their soul, or strive to deeply instill it within themselves, naturally avoid acts that are contrary to human dignity. For example, some individuals by nature will not lie or transgress the rights of others. The substance of the human celestial soul is marked by dignity, the most clear manifestation of which is one's sense of self-respect; indeed, no one welcomes humiliation. That is why in the other world, there is no harsher suffering for the human soul than to be reproached by Him (due to its neglect and misdeeds) and to experience disrespect and humiliation.

Whether we choose to believe in the existence of another world besides this one or not, death will come to us all; our real self (our soul) will leave behind our physical body and will forever remain alive. Upon death, we abandon our physical body—this heavy, dark, and stifling coat of flesh—and return to the other world (our natural habitat) to continue our life in the form of a *subtle body*, a lighter and more transparent version of our physical self.[7] There, we shall find ourselves with the same sense of self, the same general appearance, the same quality of thought, and the same level of comprehension as we had here on earth. In reality, we remain the same person we were here, only

---

7. In the interworld, each of us has a "subtle body," a semblance of our physical self in every respect. Whereas our physical body is composed of dense physical matter, our subtle body is composed of a form of extremely delicate and light "thought-matter." It should be noted that we assume a new subtle body each time we die and enter the interworld. Ostad Elahi, *Āsār ol-Haqq*, vol. 1, saying 897.

more cognizant[8] and with a deeper sense of our own dignity, without the weight of our physical body and its burdensome animalistic needs and desires.

In the interworld, the wrongs we have knowingly and intentionally committed out of evil and malice and that are recorded in our subtle body will be apparent to all; they cannot be concealed, unless He were to choose to veil or altogether suppress them. *Only by His forgiveness can one be saved.* Likewise, our good acts (such as those based on altruism or faith) will shine forth from our subtle body and be visible to all, evoking the respect and affection of others and constituting a source of pride and honor for us. The atmosphere in the hereafter is one of peace and joy, love and affection, generosity and forgiveness, with divine equity reigning supreme.

In the dignified and hierarchical societies of the other world (permeated by peace, joy, love, generosity, and dignity), the more one has accumulated spiritual provisions, practiced *living real divine truths*, and absorbed Divine light (and thus further developed one's sound reason), the closer one draws to the Source. And the closer one draws to the Source, the more radiant, honorable, able, and free one becomes, and the more intense one's ecstatic spiritual states (such as love, elation, and euphoria).

---

8. Some are more cognizant than others; the degree of this cognizance is commensurate with the thoughts and actions we adopted in this world in relation to the true God and authentic spirituality.

Chapter 9

The Functional Structure of the Human Soul
Commentary on Figure 2

> *Souls belong to different groups. Just as one blood group is incompatible with another, certain groups of souls are also incompatible with each other.*[1]

T he soul is always in a state of motion and activity, and knows no death; death and decay pertain only to the physical body. The flux of elemental souls (mineral souls) ensures the transubstantial movement of matter;[2] the flux of vegetal souls ensures plant growth; the flux of animal souls infuses animals with life; and the flux of higher-animal souls gives rise to individuated souls specific to the human embryo, which are referred to as *terrestrial souls* or *human embryonic souls*.[3] Each terrestrial soul imparts "life" to the physical body of human beings, and transfers its animal traits to the human psyche, leading to the formation the id. The combination of the terrestrial soul of a newborn and a human celestial soul forms a *human soul proper.*

---

1. Ostad Elahi, *Āsār ol-Haqq*, vol. 2, saying 194.
2. Ibid., vol. 1, saying 818.
3. This terrestrial soul, with its animal nature, instinctively and autonomously directs the intrauterine life of an embryo. That is why it is also referred to as the human embryonic soul.

Fig. 2a – Structure of the Primate Psyche

Among higher-order animals, primates are the most intelligent. Unlike humans, however, they are devoid of a celestial soul and are thus deficient with regard to celestial faculties (reason, willpower,[4] moral conscience, faith, etc.), lacking the capacity to grasp moral or spiritual issues. For primates, their soul and psyche are one and the same, resulting from the natural culminating flux of earth's *vital essence.*

Earth is a living planet that continuously gives rise to a flux of mineral souls. Under the influence of natural conditions on earth (its physical environment), and after evolving through the mineral, vegetal, and animal stages, this flux transforms into that of the souls of higher-order animals, including primates. The culmination of the flux of several higher-order animal souls results in an individuated terrestrial soul (that of a human embryo). This soul is removed from higher-order animal souls by just one degree in its process of perfection and retains the quintessential effects of all its past constituent souls (from mineral to animal). Two advantages distinguish the terrestrial soul from that of higher-order animals: (1) it is individualized, in the sense that each human embryo has its own terrestrial soul, and (2) it has the potentiality to merge with a human celestial soul so that the latter can transform into a human soul proper.

---

4. Willpower is a psychological force that originates from the human celestial soul and functions as the executive arm of reason. Through our willpower, we can resist our instincts and abstain from that which our reason disapproves of, or alternatively impose upon ourselves that which our reason approves. Willpower is thus a psychological force originating from the celestial soul of human beings that enables us to control our instincts (unlike animals, which are subservient to their instincts).

What is the Soul?

By carefully studying the writings and words of Ostad, we can conclude that the soul is a constant and inexhaustible source of vital energy, continuously emitting waves of varying frequencies similar to electromagnetic waves (waves that are not yet detectable by modern science).

At the level of the body, the soul's current of "electromagnetic" waves results in motion, life, consciousness, etc. The presence of the flux of mineral souls in particles of matter engenders transubstantial movement; the presence of the flux of vegetal souls in plants renders growth possible; the presence of the flux of animal souls imbues animals with life and emotion; the presence of the terrestrial soul in the human embryo confers human-animal life, which is expressed at the level of the psyche as the id; and the presence of the human celestial soul within the human body additionally gives rise to a form of consciousness that bears reason, faith, moral conscience, willpower, etc.

Simply put, the presence of the human soul within the human body can be likened to the presence of a battery in a humanoid robot. If its battery were disconnected or removed, the robot would cease to function, as if it were "dead." Similarly, if the soul is removed from the body and its "connectivity" to it is disrupted, the body and the brain will no longer receive the "electromagnetic" current of the soul and will cease to function, resulting in true death. Once free of the body, human souls can alter the frequency of their "electromagnetic" waves at will and—provided they are granted permission by the Source—render themselves visible to us.

Fig. 2a – Structure of the Human Psyche According to Freud

According to Freud and most psychological theories, the human soul is reduced to the psyche, which is shaped through interaction with one's environment. The principal difference between this representation of the self and Ostad's perspective is that in the former, faculties such as reason, willpower, moral conscience, and faith are thought to result from the impulses of the id and the interplay between the different structures of the psyche (the id, ego, and superego), whereas Ostad deems these faculties to originate in the human celestial soul, a soul that derives from the Source (its celestial Origin) before directly "entering" the physical body (i.e., assuming a functional[5] presence within the body that instills reason, willpower, moral conscience, faith, etc.).

Fig. 2b – Functional Structure of the Human Soul Derived from the Teachings of Ostad Elahi

In terms of its functional structure, the human soul is presented as a psychospiritual organism[6] composed of living psychospiritual faculties that are capable of evolving. In this organism, consciousness is functionally divided into two zones: the *conscious self* and the *total unconscious* (Figs. 1 and 2b). The total unconscious, in turn, is further divided into two zones: the *psychological unconscious* and the *spiritual unconscious*. Each zone of the unconscious constitutes an immense space of consciousness characterized by its own specific "wavelengths" of thought that are detectable at the level of the conscious self (Fig. 8). In

---

5. See chap. 8, note 2.
6. In biology, an organism denotes the presence of elemental constituents within a living entity.

addition to these two zones, there also exists a psychological veil, three functional membranes, and the metabrain, which collectively complete the faculties of the human soul.

1) *The Conscious Self*

Within the bubble depicting the human soul, the conscious self occupies a minute space atop the terrestrial pole. It is organized into two functional layers: the surface conscious self, or *ego*, and the deeper conscious self, or *inner guide*.

- **The ego** (surface conscious self) spontaneously saturates our mind. It is the very seat of the expression of instincts and desires stemming from *the tandem of the id and imperious self*; this tandem assumes control of our common reason and adopts it as its spokesperson. The ego constantly instills thoughts and desires of a terrestrial-animal nature in our psyche, which is why our thoughts are dominated by the imperious self.

- **The inner guide** (deeper conscious self) is a space of consciousness situated beneath the ego that can only be accessed through the sound development of one's thought. It is the site for the expression of our sound reason and the four consciences of the superego: the blaming conscience (moral conscience), the inspiring conscience, the certifying conscience, and the superid (Fig. 4).[7] The inner guide signals us, notably through the voice of our conscience (the blaming or moral conscience) and inspirations (the inspiring conscience). However, one must first learn, by soundly developing one's thought, how to listen to and

---

7. Ostad Elahi, *Borhān-ol Haqq*, 373-4.

strengthen the voice of one's conscience, and how to correctly interpret one's inspirations and make good use of them. The main role of the inner guide is to fight the imperious self with the goal of achieving complete control over the ego.

2) *The Psychological Veil*

The psychological veil is a hazy and more or less opaque layer of thought that separates our conscious self from our total unconscious. The opacity of the psychological veil is due to the activity of the tandem of the id and imperious self, especially the "dark fumes" of thought arising from the activity of the imperious self.

3) *The Total Unconscious*

The total unconscious is located beneath the psychological veil and consists of two components: the psychological unconscious and the spiritual unconscious. It comprises our entire soul, with the exception of the conscious self (Fig. 3a).

- **The psychological unconscious** consists of two functional parts: the *celestial-human part* and the *terrestrial-animal part.* The celestial-human part, or *superego* (Fig. 4a), constitutes the source of our celestial-human faculties, including reason, willpower, moral conscience, faith, etc., whereas the terrestrial-animal part, formed by the tandem of the id and imperious self, constitutes the source of terrestrial-animal traits, including pride, selfishness, callousness, aggression, the will to power, libido, revenge, etc.

- **The spiritual unconscious** occupies virtually the entirety of the total unconscious and includes the *metabrain* as well as other celestial elements and faculties, such as the *divine spark*. The effects and memories of our past lives are recorded in the spiritual unconscious, as are all of our thoughts, intentions, words, actions, and inner states, from birth till death.

4) *The Three Functional Membranes*

The psychological, spiritual, and psychospiritual membranes are living, meaning they are active and selective (Fig. 2b). These membranes are involved in regulating the exchanges between the soul (psychospiritual organism) and both its physical environment and the spiritual dimensions.

- **The psychological membrane** is involved in the exchanges between our conscious self and its earthly environment. It filters the influx of information and energy from the material world that seeks to penetrate our psyche by way of our conscious self.

  Early education, parenting, and the environment all exert a direct influence on the selectivity of this membrane. For example, the psychological membrane of one who has received a sound ethical and spiritual education (especially during youth and adolescence) is automatically more inclined to select and allow for the passage of positive information and energy from the environment into one's psyche, while resisting its negative influences. However, if the influx of negative information and energy from the environment exceeds the filtering capacity of our psychological membrane, reliance on one's faith will become necessary. Without the backbone of faith, the practice of ethics is encumbered.

Through willpower, we can impact the selectivity of our psychological membrane, making us more resilient in the face of a negative social or media environment. For example, with the help of a sound ethical and spiritual education, we can develop, by means of self-reasoning, a kind of defensive reflex that automatically devalues and rejects negative thoughts upon encountering them. Among the factors that are helpful in developing this defensive reflex are having sincere faith, socializing with positive individuals, and devoting a few minutes or more each day to the exercise of attention-dialogue.[8] But the most decisive factor in the psychological membrane's resistance to the intrusion of negative environmental influences is to have been acquainted with sound divine and ethical principles during our childhood and adolescence,[9] or to be endowed with a strong and healthy soul. The more we soundly develop our thought, the more resistant our psychological membrane becomes.

- **The spiritual membrane** is involved in the exchanges between our spiritual unconscious and the spiritual ecosphere. Sincere faith in the One (or in a true God, such as the God of an authentic monotheistic religion) positively impacts this membrane, allowing for the influx of energy from positive souls

8. For more on the exercise of attention-dialogue, see chap. 12.

9. Although easier during one's childhood and youth, it is possible to soundly develop one's thought at any age. By practicing correct divine and ethical principles, one can strengthen the resistance of one's psychological membrane to the negative influences of the environment.

or entities into our spiritual unconscious, while blocking the influx of energy from negative souls or entities. The more sincere our faith in a true God, the more effectively this membrane resists the infiltration of energy from negative entities.[10]

- **The psychospiritual membrane** is involved in the exchanges between our psychological unconscious and our spiritual unconscious. The *Point of Unicity* directly oversees the psychospiritual membrane of one who is engaged in the sound development of one's thought.

5) *The Metabrain*

The *metabrain* (the "brain" attributed to the soul) is the dominant faculty of the human soul; it reaches into the spiritual unconscious and prevails over the soul's other faculties. The biological brain, in reality, is but its instrument. As long as the soul is present within the body, the metabrain and the brain are in constant communication and interact with one another through the psyche. For example, faith in a true God, belief in the continuation of life in the hereafter, the virtues of sincerity, rectitude, compassion, beneficence, and gratefulness, as well as our impetus toward

---

10. Until such time as the existence of microbes was discovered by science, people did not know the cause of various infectious diseases or how to defend against them. Similarly, as long as we do not acknowledge the existence of saprophytic negative entities, which under certain conditions can become pathogenic for the human soul, we will not be able to defend ourselves (our soul) against them, as is currently the case. The only form of energy that can prevent saprophytic entities specific to the human soul from becoming pathogenic is one that stems from a sincere faith in a true God. When we lack faith in a true God, these saprophytic entities become pathogenic, instilling negative energy into our psyche and rendering our psyche and soul ill.

ethics all result from the influence of the metabrain upon the brain. The effects of the metabrain manifest in our conscious self through our inner guide.

The structural foundations of the metabrain are established over the course of our successive lives on earth and depend on the nature of the lifelong input our brain comes to assimilate and transmit to our metabrain via the psyche. If this input is based on *living real divine truths*, the structural foundations of our metabrain will soundly take shape; however, if this input is based on *imaginary divine truths* or *defunct truths* (truths that have lost their divine effect or active ingredient), or on truths of a purely material nature, the development of our metabrain can be stunted or impaired. Moreover, if the content of this input is spiritually toxic, it will poison our soul and render our metabrain weak and confused.

There exists between the development of the metabrain and the development of sound reason a virtuous cycle that we could call the *virtuous cycle of knowledge*: The more we develop our sound reason through the *in vivo* practice of *living real divine truths*, the better the structure of our metabrain; in turn, the better the structure of our metabrain, the more it enables the development of our sound reason. It should also be noted that a more developed common reason and intellect present more favorable grounds for the development of sound reason, provided one's attention is directed toward *living real divine truths*. Indeed, sound reason is merely a more mature form of common reason, a bidimensional reason that correctly grasps not only the material dimension of life, but also its spiritual dimension.

Just as we understand and lead our life here on earth by means of our brain, we understand and lead our life in the hereafter by means of our metabrain. Every activity that we carry out in this world using our brain, body, or external tools (technological means) can be carried out in the other world—which is composed of highly subtle "thought-matter"[11]— through the power of our thought alone and within the limits of our metabrain's willpower. Indeed, the functioning of the metabrain does not depend on any external means or tools, for it accomplishes everything through the power of its will. In the hereafter, the more developed our metabrain, the more incisive our thought, meaning that we can penetrate and come to better know the deeper layers that cover the core of a divine truth.[12]

---

11. In contrast to this world, which is composed of dense elemental matter, the other world can be said to be composed of subtle, translucent, and rarified "thought-matter," which is organized into celestial strata (heavens). The closer a stratum is to the seat of His power—the 12th heaven—the more the thought-matter that composes it is subtle, luminous, penetrating, and *effective*, and the higher the level of the souls that reside there; these souls thus enjoy greater freedom and willpower, and feel a purer divine love. As long as we are in a physical body, we find that which is material to be tangible and real. But once we assume the state of a soul, that which is composed of thought-matter becomes tangible to us instead and assumes a concrete, objective reality, while this world's material entities appear as mere shadows that can be transpierced.

12. In the hereafter, everything is true, real, and alive; nothing exists in vain. Yet, the ultimate reality (or core) of every truth is concealed by multiple onion-like layers. The more the metabrain is developed, the deeper our understanding and the greater our ability to penetrate the layers of a truth, enabling us to come closer to its true reality (core) and, to that same extent, deepen our knowledge of it. And the more our knowledge deepens, the more we experience a heightened sense of joy and marvel. For example, one's knowledge of the real truth of an authentic divine person depends on the development of one's metabrain, or in other words, the extent of the penetrating power of one's understanding. Many faithful Christians' perception of Christ in the interworld, for instance, may be distorted by their preconceptions of Christ during their lives on earth. But those who have sufficiently developed their sound reason will perceive him as he truly is. And the same holds true for adherents of the other authentic monotheistic religions.

The quality of our life in the hereafter will depend upon: (1) the amount of Divine light we absorb during our sojourn in this world by directing our attention to the One or to a true God (such as the God of an authentic monotheistic religion), (2) the amount of spiritual provisions we acquire by fighting against our imperious self and performing beneficent and charitable acts, and (3) the degree to which we develop our sound reason, and, consequently, our metabrain.

The metabrain neither ages nor forgets. It fully records and stores, in a contemporaneous manner, all the input (as well as positive and negative effects) that it processes through the brain and psyche during the course of our ascending successive lives, without ever forgetting anything.[13] In the other world, recalling the outcome of our positive thoughts and actions (such as having understood *living real divine truths* or having performed beneficent acts) will serve as a source of joy, pride, and strength, whereas recalling the outcome of our negative thoughts and actions will torment us and will constitute a source of weakness, shame, and suffering as long as He has not expunged them from our soul. In addition, the more we have developed our sound reason, and thus our metabrain, the more aware, knowing, capable, dignified, and radiant we will become, and the higher the station we will occupy (i.e., the closer our proximity to the Source), thereby enjoying greater respectability, willpower,[14] and freedom of action.

---

13. At the moment of death, we are usually connected directly to our metabrain for a brief period of "time" and all of our previous lives stream before us, as though we were reliving them in real time. Once we enter the interworld, however, we will generally forget them again, save for the last one.

14. Given that willpower is inherent to the celestial soul, everyone is endowed with it. But certain individuals are able to impose their willpower upon their ego, in which case they are said to be "strong-willed."

In general, our recognition of bliss or misfortune depends upon our reason's level of development. The appreciation of pure divine spiritual bliss and pleasure lies within the domain of our sound reason, and not our common reason. Our common reason can appreciate full well the bliss and limbic pleasures arising from the ego, but when it comes to spiritual pleasures, it can only grasp those that are admixed or coated with pleasures of a terrestrial-animal nature (limbic pseudospiritual pleasures).[15] But compared to the joyous and delightful spiritual pleasures that our sound reason is capable of grasping, limbic pseudospiritual pleasures amount to little more than candy for children. The metabrain of those who do not develop their sound reason here will not be able to truly grasp the bliss and pleasures of the hereafter; it will lack the capacity to do so. As for the ineffable exhilaration and bliss of Perfection, they can only be grasped by divine reason.

We should always bear in mind that the essential purpose of our life in this world is to complete the fundamental stage in our process of spiritual perfection, which primarily entails examining and mending our faith, sufficiently developing our sound reason, and cultivating our humanity. As a rule, the human soul can only complete this fundamental stage here in this earthly school. We should therefore strive to do our utmost to avoid having to once again return to this earthly world (to the prison of this physical body), to this site of struggle, conflict, deception, and trials of all sorts (internal battles against our imperious self and external battles with others). We would do well to also think about our life in

---

15. This stems from the fact that common reason, sound reason, and divine reason are each capable of grasping truths along a spectrum, such that lower levels of reason are incapable of grasping that which is understood by the higher levels.

the hereafter so that once we leave this body behind, we do not appear there with a weak and dysfunctional soul,[16] a confused and incapable metabrain, ashamed and disgraced. It is upon us to do what it takes here to not have to bow our heads there in shame, in a state of confusion, helplessness, and humiliation, alienated from the Source and reduced to the ranks of "sedimentary souls."[17] Such a state would create tremendous suffering for the soul (for us). If that doesn't conjure a vision of hell, then what does?

---

16. A weak and dysfunctional soul is one that is unable to impose the willpower of its celestial-human part upon its terrestrial-animal part. The essential function of a true spirituality is to thus strengthen the soul and render it functional so that we are able to impose our celestial-human part upon our terrestrial-animal part, i.e., to impose our inner guide upon our ego.

17. "Sedimentary souls" are the souls of those who, during their earthly lives, disregarded any notion of God, the soul, the hereafter, and an accounting—reducing everything to this material realm—and likewise neglected true ethics (e.g., the practice of beneficence and compassion toward those in need).

Chapter 10

The Reduced Self and Spiritual Amnesia
Commentary on Figure 3

The freer the soul from the illusory fog of passions, the thinner its amnesic veil.[1]

The *conscious self*, *regular self-consciousness*, and the *reduced self* refer to three states of the same reality within us: the conscious self refers to its static state, regular self-consciousness refers to its dynamic state, and the reduced self refers to the conscious self when it is enveloped by a layer formed of the ego's hazy thoughts and the psychological veil (Fig. 3b).

If we speak of the "reduced" self, it is to emphasize that our conscious self covers only a minimal and limited part of our soul's extremely vast field of consciousness. And yet, as long as we are in this world, it is through this reduced self that we manage our material and spiritual lives, without always realizing that we are in a state of *spiritual amnesia*.

If a spiritual path is authentic, its first task is to make us aware of our state of spiritual amnesia, and to then teach us how we can gradually emerge from this amnesic state and come to ourselves. In doing so, we will realize that there is another world besides this world and another life beyond this life, and that while engaged in an active and productive family

---

1. Ostad Elahi, *Ma'refat ol-Ruh*, 129.

and social life like others, we also have an indispensable *essential duty* to complete the fundamental stage in our process of spiritual perfection in this world. Indeed, that is the sole reason for our presence—the presence of our real self (our soul)—here on earth.

Fig. 3a – Our Real Self (Our Soul)

In this figure, the human soul proper, or our real self, is depicted as a bubble, at the top of which we find our reduced self. The reduced self is separated from the rest of the soul (its vast majority, which encompasses virtually the entirety of the bubble) by the psychological veil. The soul's field of consciousness, comparable to a small universe, is but a speck of dust in relation to the infinite field of consciousness of the One (the divine flux). And yet, the human soul's aptitude for understanding is so exceptional and vast that upon reaching Perfection, it can directly perceive and come to know the truths of both worlds commensurate with its capacity. Notwithstanding this virtually infinite aptitude for understanding, as long as we remain in this world imprisoned within our physical body, we can only access the restricted field of consciousness of our reduced self. The vast majority of us therefore live in a state of spiritual amnesia: We do not know who we really are, where we have come from, for what purpose we have been placed here, what our essential duty here is, or where we will go beyond this world and what abode (situation) awaits us there.

Regular Self-Consciousness

Our regular self-consciousness is a flux of conscious thought composed of terrestrial-animal and celestial-human thought waves; this flux shifts according to the focus of our attention. "Regular" emphasizes that in the process of spiritual perfection, we must strive to always preserve our self-consciousness in its normal (i.e., natural) state and diligently avoid entering into any altered states of consciousness that hamper our reason, for that which we observe and understand in such states is misleading and cannot be trusted. While at first the scope of our regular self-consciousness is limited to our reduced self, the potential to expand this self-consciousness is nearly infinite. Like electromagnetic waves, our self-consciousness is capable of extending throughout our soul's field of consciousness and, upon reaching Perfection, of attaining infinity; only then does our field of consciousness encompass both realms (worlds).

Fig. 3b – The Reduced Self

The reduced self refers to the conscious self when it is enveloped by a more or less thick and dark layer of the ego's hazy thoughts and the psychological veil. The negative thoughts and actions of the ego (in relation to correct divine and ethical principles) form a kind of thick, dark cognitive fog that impairs, or even completely undermines, our ability to discern Truth (including *living real divine truths*). The more our ego produces hazy thoughts and engages in negative actions, the more opacified our psychological veil becomes. This psychological veil disconnects to varying degrees our conscious self from our total unconscious (which is responsible for our communication with the spiritual dimensions), and immerses us to the same extent into a state of spiritual amnesia. Consequently, our perception of the spiritual dimension is limited to that which we perceive through our reduced self, which is next to nothing. With such a reduced and limited consciousness of the spiritual realm, how can we allow ourselves to dispute or consider as illusory such matters as the existence of God, the soul, the hereafter, and an accounting, or to even dismiss them outright and claim that physical death is the ultimate end?

At birth, a newborn lives in the conscious self of its previous life. After a few months of development, however, its present ego begins to gradually form, slowly opacifying the psychological veil and thereby forming a curtain between its conscious self and its total unconscious (the vast majority of its soul), gradually resulting in a state of spiritual amnesia. The ego is shaped by the input the psyche receives from its environment from the moment of one's birth. As such, the more this environment is spiritually barren—i.e., lacking in *living real divine truths* and rich instead in terrestrial-animal thoughts—the thicker the ego's layer of hazy thoughts, the more opacified the psychological veil, and thus the more profound one's spiritual amnesia.

Fig. 3b presents a frontal cut of our reduced self in which our conscious self is enclosed by a layer formed of the hazy thoughts of the ego and the psychological veil (see also Fig. 5). Our regular self-consciousness occupies the totality of the space of the ego, an indication that it naturally nests within the ego, while always keeping one foot within the inner guide. Consequently, it is the ego that habitually informs our thinking and way of life.

It is simple to voluntarily shift our regular self-consciousness from the ego to the inner guide: all that is required is to apply our willpower to change the quality of our thought. For example, each time we focus our attention on the omnipresence of the divine flux, on the One, or on the true God of our faith; each time we reflect on an ethical question or heed the voice of our conscience; or each time we sympathize with the misfortune of others and seek to come to their aid, etc., our regular self-consciousness immediately leaves behind the ego and shifts to the inner guide, which in turn diminishes the pride and arrogance that arises from the ego and fosters inner humility and empathy (Fig. 5). By contrast, if we neglect ethics and spirituality, the arrogance of our proud ego will spontaneously occupy the entirety of our conscious self, leaving no room for the expression of our inner guide. Our thoughts will then be dominated by our imperious self, rife with hubris and conceit. Unfortunately, such is the case for the vast majority of us.

Spiritual Amnesia

We are in a state of spiritual amnesia when our perception of spiritual realities is limited to that which we perceive through our reduced self. One of the signs we are in a state of spiritual amnesia is that when faced with material questions—which lie within the field of perception of our reduced self—we are extremely attentive and cautious so as to maximize our gains and successes, and minimize our losses and failures. Yet when it comes to spiritual matters, we remain somewhat indifferent or avoid them altogether. And if we do show an interest in such spiritual matters, we are content to blindly imitate others and are willing to believe anything or anyone, without considering the potential consequences for our soul; we seem oblivious to the fact that material gains and successes, or losses and setbacks, are finite and transient, whereas in spirituality they will endure forever.

The extent of this spiritual amnesia, however, is not the same for everyone: for some it is minimal, for others it is more profound, and in certain cases it is total. In the latter case, individuals consider reality to be limited to the physical body and the material world. They deny, sometimes derisively, God, the soul, the other world, and especially an accounting. Fortunately, most people are not in such a state: they react positively to *living real divine truths*, especially if they have benefitted from a correct ethical and spiritual education during their childhood and adolescence (in this life or in their past lives), or if they have strong and healthy souls; this is also true of those who have recently begun their cycle of earthly lives and whose soul is thus less tainted.

If we wish to actualize our innate potentials to advance along our process of spiritual perfection, we have to emerge from our state of spiritual amnesia. To do so, we must:

(1) Convince ourselves that another realm and other dimensions exist, which, like the material world, abide by the foundational principles of gravitation, opposites, causality, legitimate rights, connection, *in vivo* practice, acceptability, Divine generosity, exception . . . and that the rule of law (divine law) prevails: no one there has the desire or ability to lie, slander, transgress the rights of others, or evade the law. In the hereafter, the truth of everything becomes manifest.

(2) Know that in accordance with the principle of acceptability, if we do not do something positive for our soul here in this world, in the other world the gravitational affinity of our soul toward the Source of Truth will remain so weak—or may even assume the opposite effect and turn negative[2]—that we will

---

2. When the gravitational affinity of a person's soul toward the Source of Truth turns negative, the Source repels that soul instead of attracting it toward itself. Such a person cannot have faith, for it is God alone who grants faith.

not be accepted by any of the "heavens" occupied by spiritually-exalted entities and will have to live in "spiritual poverty" and helplessness.

(3) Understand that if we do not connect our thought to the *chain of Divine guidance* (one of the authentic monotheistic religions) and/or *Divine guidance*[3] while here on earth, we will find ourselves alone and lost over there, unless we had sincerely observed true ethics and practiced beneficence, in which case the Creator will still come to our aid.

Therefore, to emerge from this state of spiritual amnesia, we must, if only as an experiment, temporarily set aside our pride and superioritism in relation to divine truths, and strive to act as research scientists would in relation to the truths of their science. For the spirituality that leads the human soul to Perfection is an experimental science, a new medicine of the soul—one of self-knowledge and the knowledge of God within us—that can only be understood and learned through one's sound reason. Thus, to begin we must sufficiently develop our sound reason through the *in vivo* practice of correct divine and ethical principles, coupled with a few minutes or more of the daily exercise of attention-dialogue.[4] As our sound reason gradually develops, we can rise, like a chick breaking through its shell, from the shell of spiritual ignorance of our reduced self and establish a stronger connection with our total unconscious,

---

3. Whereas the *chain of Divine guidance* is intended for humanity at large and falls under the purview of the authentic monotheistic religions (whose aim is to lead one to paradise), *Divine guidance* speaks to those whose souls have spiritually advanced such that they automatically seek the Truth and have set Perfection as their goal.

4. See chap. 12.

which is in direct communication with the spiritual realm. Note that in the experimental sciences, if we limit ourselves to purely theoretical research without conducting *in vivo* experimentation, we will not be able to grasp the truths of our science. By analogy, when it comes to God and spirituality, if we limit ourselves to theoretical research, without applying *living real divine truths in vivo*—that is, in the midst of society and through interaction with others—we will not be able to grasp their reality and will become mired in pointless and futile intellectual philosophical discourse, or worse, be drawn to misguided spiritual paths whose prescriptions cater to the ego (by seeking more adherents in order to amass greater profit).

The stronger our inner connection with our total unconscious becomes, the less profound the state of our spiritual amnesia. One of the first signs of establishing this connection is that we begin to earnestly contemplate God and spirituality and worry about our destiny in the hereafter, determined to do something while here so that we do not return there empty-handed.

For What Purpose Are We Here?

No being is either mature or perfect at its creation, and the human celestial soul is no exception. The celestial soul can be likened to a young school-age student in that it has been temporarily separated from its home (Origin) and sent to the school of earthly life—assuming one or more physical bodies—to complete the fundamental stage in its process of spiritual perfection. Thereafter, the soul acquires the requisite acceptability to continue with the advanced stage[5] in its process of

---

5. See chap. 13.

spiritual perfection in the interworld, no longer having to return to this world of amnesia, deception, trials, and conflict to once again live in amnesia amidst the amnesic.

The primary duty of the authentic monotheistic religions (the *chain of Divine guidance*) is to cultivate the seed of faith in the unique God, to instill belief in the existence of the soul, the hereafter, and an accounting, and to teach the foundations of morality, in particular respect for legitimate rights (especially those of others) and the practice of beneficence (particularly toward one's fellow beings). In short, their mission is to bring people to observe God's commands as well as the hygiene of their body, psyche, and soul, thereby leading to the germination of the seed of sound reason (found within the common reason of all human beings). Thereafter, this germinated seed takes root within the soul and becomes part of its genetic makeup, always staying with it during the course of its future successive lives and resulting in an innate and spontaneous attraction toward God and/or true ethics.

Once the seed of sound reason has germinated, it is up to each of us to decide whether or not to embark on the fundamental stage in the process of spiritual perfection. Following this decision, in accordance with the principle of connection, it becomes necessary to connect our thought to *Divine guidance*. The latter does not impose the adoption of any prescriptions or principles upon anyone, but rather makes *living real divine truths* accessible to those who seek them. These truths, along with Divine light and spiritual provisions, constitute the essential nutrients of the human soul and allow for its development.

By virtue of our reason and free will, we have but one essential spiritual duty while living in this world: to diligently engage in our process of spiritual perfection in order to complete its fundamental stage here on earth. "Duty" in this context does not imply outward compulsion—nor should there be any—but rather refers to self-compulsion. Thus, as long as we are living here on earth, we are free to pursue our process of spiritual perfection or not. Given that our spiritual amnesia is lifted in the hereafter, those of us who have chosen to ignore our spiritual perfection will suddenly come to ourselves and behold our lamentable state in comparison to others: We will then seek to plead for His help from the depths of our being to grant us a second chance. And yet some will find they are incapable of calling out to Him despite wanting to do so. As a result of having only cultivated and strengthened the terrestrial-animal faculties of their psyche instead of their celestial-human faculties, they have become afflicted with a kind of "paralysis" of the metabrain (the center of decision-making relating to celestial-human thoughts).

Any physical or psychospiritual organ or faculty that is not exercised will gradually weaken and become dysfunctional. For example, if one of our limbs is immobilized in a cast for an extended period, the atrophy from the lack of exercise will lead to its dysfunction for some time. Similarly, if we completely reject the concept of God, the soul, and the hereafter, and thus fail to exercise here the faculties of the celestial-human part of our psyche that animate the inner guide, the paralytic dysfunction of these faculties will become apparent in the hereafter and we will suffer greatly from this disability.[6]

Once in the hereafter, we will each reap the fruits of the positive or negative acts, words, and thoughts we have sown in this world. To deny the existence of God, the soul, the hereafter, and an accounting is as futile

---

6. Understanding that the soul by nature is in a perpetual state of activity and motion allows us to better visualize and appreciate the hardship and suffering it experiences (we experience) from this paralytic state of willpower.

as denying death. Regardless of what we believe, all of us will eventually succumb to death: Our physical body will expire and decompose, but our soul (our real self) will always remain alive and intact. Indeed, by virtue of our reason and free will, we will have to answer for our thoughts, words, and actions during our stay on earth, which were contemporaneously recorded in our soul.

Where Do We Go After This World?

Upon death, we leave behind our physical body—this heavy, dark, and stifling coat of flesh—and return to the interworld in the form of a *subtle body*. At the same time, our psychological veil dissipates, such that our conscious self and our total unconscious become one. We then come to realize with amazement the potential immensity of our field of consciousness, of which we had been oblivious during our life on earth.

Immediately upon leaving our body, we find ourselves at the threshold of the interworld. For the souls of beings on earth, this interworld is a temporary abode in continuum with this earthly world, only of a higher dimension and of greater immensity and beauty. Situated between this world and the permanent spiritual worlds, the interworld is made of subtle and transparent "thought-matter" that nonetheless has a more tangible, penetrating, and impactful[7] *effect* than that of heavier and denser earthly matter.

---

7. More "impactful" implies a greater impact on the mind and the senses, one that is more powerful, tangible, and concrete than earthly matter and thus penetrates our being more profoundly. For example, a fruit in the interworld is more beautiful, fragrant, and delicious than that same fruit here on earth. Everything in the interworld mostly resembles what we find here, with the difference that it produces a deeper and more penetrating impact on our being.

The environment in the interworld is so similar to our own earthly environment that we do not feel estranged there. Everything is alive, transparent, beautiful, luminous, and joy-inducing. Moreover, everyone enjoys a greater sense of well-being, even those who find themselves in its lower levels, such that one rarely wishes to return and assume a new physical body. In the interworld, the reality of each person is revealed, and no one can lie, cheat, conceal anything, falsely accuse others, or transgress rights. Order and accountability prevail, as do fairness and Divine generosity. The feeling of the presence of the divine flux fills the heart with love, joy, and a sense of security.

We manifest in the interworld in the form of our subtle body—a replica of our earthly body—with the same appearance, "mental baggage," and knowledge we had acquired here on earth. Our level of understanding there will be contingent upon the level of development of our sound reason, while our situation will depend on the quality of our thoughts, words, and actions during our stay on earth, as well as the amount of spiritual provisions accumulated and Divine light absorbed. If we were benevolent and came to the aid of those in need, we will be well received and will buoyantly and joyously join our true loved ones.[8] If we also had sincere faith in a true God, the flux of His presence will become more palpable to us; in exceptional cases, at the moment of death it is even possible for a person of sincere faith to behold Him if only for an instant, leading to a sense of ineffable metacausal ecstasy. Better still, if we have acquired the acceptability to remain in the interworld, we will enjoy far more favorable learning conditions and can readily put into

---

8. Our true loved ones are those whose souls are close to and compatible with us. Whether in this world or in the other, true loved ones are drawn to and sincerely love each other.

practice the *living real divine truths* we are taught. In reality, so much better are the living conditions that earthly life by comparison appears like a prison. As such, virtually no one (no soul) is willingly prepared to return to life on earth.

By contrast, the plight of those who were malevolent or transgressive, or who shunned correct divine and ethical principles and frequently infringed upon the rights of others, will be anything but enviable. Worse still is the state of those who committed *spiritual crimes*[9]—for example, having assumed the position of a spiritual guide without direct approval from the Source of Truth, or having disseminated toxic (anti-divine or unethical) ideologies for the satisfaction of their own ego, untethering people and leading them adrift. Such individuals will find themselves in an extremely undesirable condition, stricken by a deep sense of shame and profound anxiety.

Apart from these specific cases, however, death is experienced by most people as a rebirth, as though they were liberated from prison, accompanied by a feeling of buoyancy and joy. There, one experiences to varying degrees the divine love and peace of mind that stem from the flux of His presence (the divine flux), even if perceived only as a faint glimmer.

Again, whether we believe the interworld exists or not, all of us will eventually return there. The interworld resembles this world, only it is more limpid, clear, lively, rational, and far more active; everyone there is engaged in activity. In that world, the rule of law in its true sense prevails, which no one is able, nor wishes, to defy. The smallest details of all our thoughts (in particular our intentions), words, and actions on earth are

---

9. A spiritual criminal is one who drives people away from the Truth by using religion and spirituality as a means to obtain celebrity, power, wealth, or sex.

recorded and accounted for over there, just as they are within our own being; nothing is omitted. Fortunately, we also benefit from His ever-present generosity and benevolence. Everything may be forgiven, except for the transgressions of others' rights, especially if those transgressions were knowingly and intentionally committed and no effort was made to make amends and/or to seek forgiveness.

Of all the things that we can take with us to the interworld, the most beneficial are sincere faith in a true God (a correct faith) and/or good deeds and genuine beneficent acts. As for the increasing number of people who cannot rationally come to accept God as advanced by the religions of today, if they abide by true ethics and practice beneficence without any pretense, this dilemma will be resolved for them once they are in the interworld.

Why Believe In An Accounting?

When we recognize that everything we do here in this world, whether good or bad, is fully recorded within our own being and in the other world, we become more observant of the rights of others. Indeed, human nature is such that we tend not to control ourselves if we do not fear some consequence. The knowledge that we will face an accounting of our thoughts and actions, and that no right can ultimately be infringed, generates within us what can be called a "fear of God." The question of belief in an accounting is a highly consequential one and should be approached with precision, for no one is exempt from it. Our entire life—including our thoughts, intentions, words, and inner states—from the moment of birth until death, is fully and contemporaneously recorded within our soul (psychospiritual organism), such that on the day of our "accounting," we will be unable to conceal or disavow anything. All our good deeds, no matter how minute, will be taken into account, as will all those acts that run counter to correct divine and ethical principles, including and especially those committed knowingly and intentionally.

Each time we die, we necessarily return to our earth's interworld, where all the information recorded in our soul is reproduced live and serves as the basis of our accounting and the determination of our future destiny. One should know that attitudes of dismissal, rejection, or even disparagement of the belief in an accounting stem from the total dominance of the imperious self over the psyche.

Chapter 11

The Psyche and the Human Soul
Commentary on Figure 4

Fig. 4a – The Human Psyche

T he human psyche, which constitutes only one part of the soul, is a small mental space that allows for the brain-soul connection. It is specific to each individual, such that no two psyches are completely identical. From the moment of birth, our brain is constantly under the influence of two fluxes of thought—emotional thoughts and cognitive thoughts—that originate from two primary sources: the body and its earthly environment; the soul and the other world. These two fluxes of thought continuously enter the brain and encode it as if it were a "biological" computer. Upon receiving these two fluxes of thought, the brain imprints them with its own specific effects before transferring them to the psyche. Thus, the psyche can be analogized to a "mental lake" into which these two tributaries of thought constantly flow, determining the quality of its water. Each person's quality of life—in this world and in the hereafter—is directly linked to the quality of water in this mental lake, for the waters of this mental lake are the source of nourishment for the soul, much like the waters of a lake are for a fish.

The psyche is formed from the concentration of dissolved quintessential elements (properties) of the terrestrial soul within the terrestrial pole of the human soul proper (Fig. 4b). The formation of the psyche is necessary for the human celestial soul, for it is through the psyche (and the brain) that the soul can interact with, and receive nourishment from, its earthly environment. In figurative terms, the psyche functions like an elephant's trunk: It culls nutrients from the earthly environment and transfers them to the soul.

The psyche is composed of the conscious self and the psychological unconscious.

1) *The Conscious Self*

The conscious self is composed of the ego (or surface conscious self) and the inner guide (or deeper conscious self), and continuously emits a flux of thought arising from our *regular self-consciousness*. This flux of thought is primarily a mixture of thought waves of a terrestrial-animal nature emitted by the ego, and thought waves of a celestial-human nature emitted by the inner guide. These two types of thought waves are supplemented by various thoughts that arise from our earthly environment as well as inspirations that arise from the other world.

During the course of its ascending successive lives, each time the human soul assumes a new body it is endowed with a new psyche, and thus with a new conscious self. In addition to its own specific character traits, this new psyche also inherits a number of conspicuous characteristics (positive or negative) from its past psyche(s), such as the germinated seed of sound reason, or a spontaneous attraction or aversion toward the notion of God or certain individuals or things. However, its initial sense of self, which the soul acquires upon assuming a body for the first time, remains forever unchanged. In reality, during the course of its successive lives, it is this same self that passes from one body to the next, just as it is this same self that appears in the other world and is held to account.

2) *The Psychological Unconscious*

The psychological unconscious is divided into two functional parts: a terrestrial-animal part and a celestial-human part.

(a) **The terrestrial-animal part of the psychological unconscious** is composed of the *id* and the *imperious self,* which together assume control of our common reason (Fig. 4a). The id and the imperious self, aided by our common reason, give rise to impulses and desires of a terrestrial-animal nature that constantly surface in our ego and absorb our thoughts (Fig. 7). As our *regular self-consciousness* nests within the ego—we habitually think through our ego—all of our thoughts are naturally under the influence of the impulses and desires of our terrestrial-animal part, especially the imperious self (Fig. 3b). Indeed, the thought of all human beings is generally dominated by their imperious self, except those who are actively engaged in fighting against it.

The id (our pure animal nature) instinctively supports the biological aspect of human life. Its level of reason does not exceed that of a small child and it primarily derives its energy from libido and the will to power. The id lies at the origin of our purely animal character traits and instincts.[1] Like an animal, it solely obeys its instincts and has no real conceptual understanding of

---

1. These include, among others, the instinct of survival, the sexual instinct, the reproductive instinct, hunger and sleep, the search for pleasure and the avoidance of pain, territoriality, anger and fear, and fight or flight.

such notions as faith, good and evil, self-interest or detriment, nor does it recognize any limits of a divine or ethical nature. Without the help of the inner guide, the character traits of the id will lapse into disequilibrium (to either extreme) and become misguided, transforming into weak points or character flaws within us. When these weak points or character flaws become active, they automatically produce the imperious self.

The imperious self is an extremely powerful psychological energy that is harmful to the soul and leads one toward thoughts and actions that are contrary to correct divine and ethical principles. In human beings, weak points relate either to divine or ethical principles. For example, dismissing the notion of God, the soul, the hereafter, and an accounting are weak points or flaws in relation to divine principles, whereas cruelty, aggression, the transgression of others' rights, lying, malevolence, misplaced pride,[2] etc., are character weak points or flaws in relation to ethical principles.

To diagnose (identify) a character weak point or flaw, we must properly understand and keep in mind correct divine and ethical principles (which are part of *living real divine truths*) as a frame of reference. In effect, a character weak point or flaw arises when a character imbalance exceeds the limits established by these correct divine and ethical principles. Whether such an excess is deemed an offense depends upon the level of development

---

2. Misplaced pride is one that engenders arrogance and superioritism within us, whereas pride that engenders dignity and self-esteem is necessary and useful. For instance, young people with self-esteem, i.e., who respect their own human dignity, will always advance and succeed in life.

of one's sound reason: The more developed one's sound reason, the greater one's spiritual responsibility. Thus, a negative act or thought toward another person that is not deemed blameworthy at a given stage in the process of spiritual perfection can be counted as a misdeed at a higher stage. For instance, early in the process of spiritual perfection, one may not be held accountable for unrealized negative thoughts, but at more advanced levels, these very thoughts will be counted against us.

The legitimate impulses and desires of the id are at the root of our instinct of survival and spur us to take an interest in our material lives. These impulses and desires are quite important and beneficial to our process of spiritual perfection, for it is only within the school of earthly life that we can complete the fundamental stage in this process—namely, examining and mending our faith (directing it toward a true God), sufficiently developing our sound reason, and cultivating our humanity, such that it dominates our animal nature. But to succeed in dominating our animality, we must refuse—and when possible, subdue and neutralize—the impulses and desires of our imperious self with the help of the metacausal energy of the One (which is harnessed through a sincere faith). In reality, if we leave the impulses and desires of our imperious self—which reinforce our animality—to their own devices, they will be extremely harmful for our soul and will drag it down, impeding our process of spiritual perfection. On the other hand, if we are unable to completely neutralize these impulses and desires but persist in fighting against them, they will prove to be of great benefit, for it is precisely this ongoing struggle against the imperious self that enables us to develop our sound reason and, with it, our soul, thereby allowing us to advance in our process of spiritual perfection.

Causal Charges

A causal charge refers to any character weak point or flaw (relating to a divine or ethical principle) that engenders a subjugating psychological attachment to material values (money, power, sex, fame, kinship, progeny, etc.), such that we feel incapable of confronting it alone and find ourselves desperate and helpless in relation to it, as with virtually all forms of addiction or disorders that paralyze one's willpower.

The most common causal charges are the subjugating attachment to progeny, money, and power. An unrestrained causal charge prevents us from advancing in our process of spiritual perfection. Without the direct support of the One or the *Point of Unicity*, the fight against causal charges can prove to be extremely difficult, if not impossible. But we will only receive this support if we are constantly engaged in a struggle against our causal charges; even if we suffer numerous defeats, we must persist in this fight until eventually the One or the *Point of Unicity* directly comes to our aid. Certain causal charges that produce a form of severe mental addiction may also benefit from psychotherapy, for advancement in the process of spiritual perfection requires a healthy and balanced psyche.

(b) **The celestial-human part of the psychological unconscious**, or the *superego*, is composed of four consciences or psychological faculties of a celestial nature: the *certifying, inspiring,* and *blaming consciences*, as well as the *superid* (Fig. 4a). Once a human celestial soul assumes a psychical state (meaning that it transforms into a human soul proper), the reasoning specific to these four consciences becomes bidimensional (i.e., prone to excess or deficiency and to being misguided) and thus educable (Fig. 4b). What characterizes these four consciences is an inherent attraction toward divine truths and beneficence, and an aversion toward anything to the contrary. They also nourish our inner guide and are at the service of our sound reason. In practice, it is through our inner guide that the feelings and voices arising from these four consciences, as well as the directives of our sound reason, manifest.

These four consciences are each tasked with a specific function in the psychospiritual organism (much like the functional regions of the physical brain). They are simultaneously in contact and interaction with various constituents of the soul. For example, when we perform a deed that is in accord with divine contentment, the certifying conscience certifies that God is pleased with our action and instills within our heart and mind a momentary feeling of inner certitude and reassurance, imbued with a particular sense of euphoria. In the case of the inspiring conscience, it is the means by which we receive inspirations from the spiritual world, but we must learn through the use of our sound reason to analyze and select those that are accurate and beneficial.[3] As for our blaming (or moral) conscience, it is

3. Not all inspirations originate from the Source or from positive entities; certain circumstances allow for harmful inspirations from negative entities as well. Given the potential harm to the human soul, we must therefore analyze our

what gives rise to one's voice of conscience. If this conscience is to function correctly and to be reliable, however, it is absolutely essential that it be developed with correct divine and ethical principles. Only then will it blame us when we act contrary to such principles, in which case its voice must be heeded; in the absence of such an education, it cannot be deemed fully reliable. Finally, the superid is a reservoir of spiritual impulses, such as the impulse to worship (faith) and the impulse to seek truth. Our inner guide must steer these impulses in the right direction with the help of our sound reason.

Just as the faculties of the id can lapse into excess and even become misguided, so too can the faculties of the superego, resulting in harm to the soul. Here again, it is up to our sound reason to control the four faculties of the superego— the certifying, inspiring, and blaming consciences, as well as the superid—and to preserve their functional equilibrium. An uncontrolled superego, for example, could lead to mystical excess, which, in fragile minds, can bring about "spiritual megalomania," the pursuit of supernatural powers, and "mystical delirium." On the other hand, those who are engaged in their process of spiritual perfection and have sufficiently developed their sound reason behave in a normal and sensible manner; they do not flaunt their spiritual states. Indeed, a spirituality that leads toward Perfection is an inner and reflective process, one that must be directed by our sound reason.

---

inspirations with the aid of our sound reason to identify those that are in fact sound and beneficial.

In general, the process of spiritual perfection requires that our inner guide, with the help of our sound reason, constantly monitor the id and the four faculties of the superego to ensure that they do not lapse into a state of functional disequilibrium. Yet our main effort should remain directed toward controlling the ego and neutralizing the imperious self. *Perfection is reached when our inner guide acquires total mastery over our ego, and our sound reason is transmuted into divine reason by the One.*

There is a constant conflict between the faculties of the terrestrial-animal part and those of the celestial-human part of our psychological unconscious that manifests at the level of our conscious self in the form of feelings such as remorse or a guilty conscience, and at times as a concern for our life in the hereafter (our spiritual destiny). This inner conflict is essential to the dynamic of our process of spiritual perfection, for without it there would be no *inner dialogue* between our ego and our inner guide, and the *cognitive flux of thoughts* pertaining to ethics and spirituality would not circulate within our conscious self (Fig. 7). Absent this flux, our thoughts would not gravitate toward the domain of ethics or spirituality, nor would there be any process of spiritual perfection to speak of.

If we do not concern ourselves with spirituality and do not make any effort to strengthen our celestial-human dimension, this confrontation between the two parts of our psychological unconscious will spontaneously persist until the terrestrial-animal part comes to subdue the celestial-human part. Indeed, if we do not actively harness the dynamic of this inner conflict to control our terrestrial-animal faculties, the latter will automatically and instinctively dominate our celestial-human faculties, thereby silencing our inner guide. The imperious self will then seize control of our reason and reign supreme over our entire psyche (Fig. 8c).

If there are some who do not feel the effects of this inner conflict within them (such as the voice of their conscience or concern for their spiritual destiny), or do not feel empathy or compassion for others, or do not ask themselves whether God, the soul, the hereafter, and an accounting exist, it is because their terrestrial-animal faculties have subjugated and "stifled" their celestial-human faculties. Those who are in such a state have lost all conventional notions of good and evil[4] and are instead solely preoccupied with the quest for selfish pleasures, convinced that there remains nothing beyond death. The voice of their conscience has become impaired and dysfunctional; they transgress the rights of others without any compunction and commit all sorts of inhumane acts that are contrary to divine and ethical principles, without feeling the slightest remorse. In reality, they bear the appearance of a human—they may even enjoy a certain respectability and popularity—but their psyche is comparable to that of a primate: They lack belief in a God, a soul, a hereafter, or an accounting, and have not mentally assimilated correct ethical principles. Such individuals are harmful to themselves and others, often prone to paranoia and bouts of recurring anxiety and depression. And if they happen to take an interest in religion or spirituality, it is their own pleasure that they seek and the recognition of others (at any cost) rather than divine contentment.

---

4. Conventional notions of good and evil have been fully set forth and elaborated upon by the authentic monotheistic religions and sincere moralists. At their core, these notions remain unchanged over time.

Fig. 4b – The Human Soul Proper (The Psychical State)

The first time a human celestial soul is introduced into the body of a newborn (upon its first breath) and the quintessential properties of the newborn's terrestrial soul are dissolved within it, the celestial soul assumes a *psychical state*, i.e., a psyche with a sense of self appears within it. The human celestial soul, which is unidimensional, thus permanently transforms into a *human soul proper*, which is bidimensional, and thereby becomes functional. This can be likened to dissolving ink in pure water, which then takes on the character of the ink.

While endowed at its creation with a celestial intelligence of great aptitude, the human celestial soul is nonetheless unidimensional. Because this intelligence is limited only to that which is "good" and "positive," it is incapable of distinguishing between opposites, and does not allow for *selfish egoity*; as such, it is not yet functional. Thus, prior to combining with a terrestrial soul and assuming a psychical state, the human celestial soul cannot undertake its process of perfection or acquire self-knowledge. In addition, the soul's sensorial faculties of sight, smell, hearing, taste, touch, etc., remain only as potentialities, and it cannot assume a *subtle body* to render itself perceptible. However, once the human celestial soul assumes a psychical state and becomes complete (bidimensional and functional), the following changes take place: (1) the sensory faculties of sight, hearing, etc., become actualized within it; (2) it becomes capable of assuming a subtle body and thus rendering itself perceptible; (3) its celestial intelligence becomes bidimensional and results in the formation of reason (common reason), which makes it capable of distinguishing between opposites as well as benefit and harm; and (4) along with the emergence of reason, a sense of self and non-self (the other) becomes apparent within it, as do *selfish egoity* and inner conflict.

Selfish egoity refers to the impulse to give preference to oneself in relation to all that one deems good. Egoity can be either positive or negative: if it is transformed into the *will to transcendence*, it is considered positive and beneficial for the soul; on the other hand, if it is transformed into *exclusionary selfishness, insatiable greed*, or the *insatiable will to power* under the influence of the imperious self, it is deemed negative and harmful for the soul. When we turn toward spirituality and true ethics, this selfish egoity transforms into the *will to transcendence*, driving us ever-higher toward the Source of transcendence. Our sound reason, by drawing upon this will to transcendence, will then lead us to come to know ourselves and to know God. By contrast, in those who are subjugated by their imperious self and who dismiss spirituality and true ethics, the imperious self transforms selfish egoity into insatiable greed (financial, sexual, etc.) and/or the insatiable will to power. Similar to diabetes insipidus where one's thirst is unquenchable, the insatiable will to power is such that the more power one has, the more one thirsts for it. Indeed, history bears witness to the many ills that have befallen humanity arising from this insatiable will to power.

Chapter 12

The Exercise of Attention-Dialogue
Commentary on Figure 5

> *To focus your attention during prayer,
> imagine that you are delivering a speech to
> a large audience; you would be cognizant of
> the meaning of your words before they were
> uttered. And to maintain your concentration,
> imagine that you are before God and He is
> listening to you.*[1]

The consciousness of the One is like a "light"[2] that radiates upon and within all existent beings through the divine flux.[3] This divine flux, which is imbued with His thought, power, and will, is omnipresent, enveloping and penetrating the whole of creation. For beings, existence, consciousness, and understanding are dependent on this radiating light; if He wills for this light to no longer radiate within a being, the latter would instantly return to nothingness. The "amount" of Divine light that a being can absorb is commensurate with the capacity of its soul.

---

1. Ostad Elahi, *Paroles de Vérité*, saying 35.
2. Divine light bears metacausal energy and confers the discernment of Truth. Metacausal energy reinforces our faith, rendering our soul alert and active, while the inoculation of our soul with the discernment of Truth helps develop our sound reason.
3. For more on the divine flux, see chap. 1.

The capacity of the human soul to absorb Divine light is so great that it is possible, through one's efforts, to complete one's *knowledge of Truth* and thus reach the threshold of Perfection. By contrast, in those subjugated by their ego, the imperious self will cause them to regress to the basest of levels; in certain exceptional cases, their soul may even lose its divine spark and become worthless "residue," which would be tantamount to reverting to a form of nothingness (Fig. 6).

The foundational principles of gravitation and causality[4] make it incumbent upon us—as part of our essential duty—to turn our attention toward the One, or toward a true God, to merit the right to have Him look upon us. Each time that He looks upon us, our soul absorbs a certain amount of Divine light. But if we do not compel ourselves to turn our attention toward Him, we should not expect Him to look upon us either. Indeed, He will not do so, for it would be contrary to His justice— contrary to the foundational principles of gravitation and causality that He Himself has established—to look upon beings endowed with reason and free will if they have not performed their essential duty of turning their attention toward Him. He acts toward us (beings endowed with reason and free will) as we act toward Him. One of the practices that can help us actively turn our attention toward Him, or a true God, is the *exercise of attention-dialogue*.

Some Preliminary Observations

- What is referred to as "attention-dialogue" here is not a

---

4. See chap. 1. The principle of causality constitutes one of the main pillars of His justice and equity. Without this principle, divine justice and equity would be nothing more than words, devoid of any tangible reality.

prescribed ritual,[5] but rather a form of universal prayer and invocation that can be practiced by anyone sincerely seeking the Truth, regardless of individual beliefs or culture.

- We should bear in mind that we live through our *reduced self* and are thus in a state of spiritual amnesia to varying degrees. Although our regular self-consciousness generally nests within our ego (our surface conscious self), it constantly shifts between the ego and the inner guide (our deeper conscious self) (Figs. 3b and 5). This back and forth reveals itself as a fluctuation in the quality of our thought: When turning our attention within, a preoccupation with terrestrial-animal thoughts (the daily concerns of earthly life) is indicative that our regular self-consciousness at that moment lies within our ego. By contrast, a preoccupation with celestial-human thoughts (concerns of an ethical or spiritual nature) indicates that our regular self-consciousness at that moment has temporarily descended into our inner guide. Thus, each time we actively turn our attention toward the One, or recall and reflect upon *living real divine truths* that we have learned and apply such truths in an *in vivo* manner, or contemplate altruistic thoughts, the divine omnipresence (the divine flux), the existence of the soul, our situation in the hereafter, etc., we are automatically situated in our inner guide, for it is from there that such thoughts originate.

- When performing the exercise of attention-dialogue, we should keep in mind that by nature the impulses and desires of the ego stand in opposition to those of the inner guide. It is as

5. Hence, this exercise is not incompatible with the formal prayers of the religions.

if the ego were engaged in a game of yo-yo with our regular self-consciousness. Each time we exercise willpower to impose correct divine and ethical thoughts upon ourselves in order for our regular self-consciousness to descend into our inner guide, the ego immediately seizes our thoughts and imprints them with its own terrestrial-animal concerns. This yo-yo-like movement can be detected by the immediate changes that manifest in the quality of our thoughts. Until such time as the inner guide has gained sufficient strength to assume control over the ego, this game of yo-yo will persist and the ego will almost always prevail.

The Exercise of Attention-Dialogue

"Attention" consists in mentally delving within (the bubble of our soul) and focusing on the One, either directly or indirectly through the channel of the God of our faith (provided He is true), or through the channel of an Essence-bearing *Presence*. "Dialogue" refers to conversing with the One in the language of our inner guide (Fig. 5).

Regardless of individual beliefs or cultures, those who regularly practice this exercise, even for just a few minutes a day,[6] will tangibly experience its positive effects. As for those who do not believe in any God and do not follow any religion, but are sincerely in search of Truth, they too can try this exercise purely on an experimental basis. Provided that they sincerely concentrate on the "Source of Truth" with humility and

---

6. There are some who devise a regular program based on specific times throughout the day. For example, three or more times daily at noon, sunset, and night (post-sunset till dawn). A regular program of attention-dialogue has the benefit of gradually fostering the habit of being in a state of *constant attention*. In addition, it promotes discipline and strengthens one's willpower.

respect, and practice this exercise for a sufficient period of time, they will tangibly experience its positive effects, to the point that it will change their outlook on life and this world.

In the following sections, we will examine: (1) the attention phase, (2) the dialogue phase, and (3) the conditions for the exercise of attention-dialogue.

1) *The Attention Phase*

The attention phase involves focusing within and mentally entering the bubble of our soul with the intention of establishing a connection and engaging in a dialogue with the One (the Source of Truth), or with the God of an authentic monotheistic religion.[7] The space within this bubble of consciousness is so immense that it appears infinite to us. Within this "infinite" space, we must adopt humility—that is, we must envision ourselves as a microscopic being, a mere particle (Fig. 5). As our intention in mentally entering the bubble of our soul is to engage in a dialogue with the One, we will automatically be situated in the space of our inner guide upon entering the bubble.

Within the space of our inner guide—and while continuing to mentally envision ourselves in the "infinite" space of our soul—we must try to immediately concentrate on the One by means of the divine flux and directly establish an inner connection with Him. If we find it

---

7. The Gods of the authentic monotheistic religions all stem from the Source of Truth and are together merged into the One. The history of religion refers to some of these true Gods: the God of Adam, the God of Noah, the God of Abraham, the God of Zoroaster, the God of Moses, the God of Jesus, and the God of Muhammad. From our standpoint, all are true and receive their mission from the Source of Truth. As for the historical Buddha, who but a true God was the source of his illumination and awakening?

challenging to concentrate on the One, who is infinite, we can exercise our willpower to choose a Presence (provided it truly bears the Essence) to envision before us and focus upon to prevent our thought from wandering; we can then engage in a dialogue with the One (the Infinite) through the divine flux. From that moment onward, the ego seeks to seize back our thoughts and imprint them with its own terrestrial-animal preoccupations; in response, we must draw upon our willpower to repeatedly redirect our thought back to our inner guide in order to continue our dialogue with the One. This yo-yo-like game will continue until our inner guide has assumed sufficient control over our ego. As long as we are able to maintain our celestial-human thoughts through the use of our willpower, we will remain in the space of our inner guide and will be able to continue our dialogue (our heart-to-heart) with the One, irrespective of where we are or what we are doing (whether seated, lying down, walking, etc.).[8] What matters is to have our attention directed toward the One (the Infinite). Over time, the more our inner guide is able to control the ego, the longer we are able to sustain our attention on the One. The more our attention is accompanied by heartfelt emotion, the better our words will reach their intended target and the more Divine light our soul will absorb.

Before we select who to focus upon as a Presence, it is essential to carefully reflect upon the principle of connection.[9] In doing so, a proper assessment will certainly result in choosing as our focal point one who

---

8. "God will accept any individual, intimate prayer, regardless of the time, place, manner, quality, and purpose . . . provided that one's attention is directed toward the Source." Ostad Elahi, *Āsār ol-Haqq*, vol. 1, saying 526.
9. See chap. 1, "The Principle of Connection."

truly bears the Essence.[10] The Presence that we choose must bear the Essence if it is to be connected to the One and thus capable of amplifying and directly transmitting our messages to Him; otherwise, this presence will act like a non-conductive cable or an amplifier that is disconnected from a power source and our messages will fail to reach the One.

It is extremely important to recognize that the hierarchy of spiritual stations and levels borders on the infinite. It is possible for some in this world to enjoy considerable fame and publicity and to thus be perceived as occupying a high spiritual station and status, worthy of being a presence to focus upon, though in reality they are but products of the media and have little or no value or influence in the other world. Conversely, it may be that a person chooses to live a discrete life while occupying the highest of spiritual stations in the other world, as did the *Point of Unicity* during his life on earth. The first instance refers to an imaginary truth—we incorrectly imagine such persons to have true spiritual power—whereas the second refers to an all-powerful real Truth that lies beyond our imagination.

In choosing this Presence, some envision and focus upon the God of their religion, others envision one of His manifestations (theophanies), and still others envision one of the prophets or saints. Provided that the Presence chosen as a point of concentration is true, i.e., that it bears the Essence, they are on the right track and the Creator will lead them toward the goal promised them by the prophet or saint of their faith

---

10. Examples include the founding prophets of the authentic monotheistic religions and some of the great saints. An Essence-bearer refers to one who permanently bears and manifests a more or less substantial "amount" of Divine light. On this subject, see chap. 3.

(paradise, for example). But Perfection is a different matter:[11] We must know each real divine truth in its own place and as it actually is, not as we imagine it to be.

Those whose sound reason has sufficiently developed and are sincerely in pursuit of the Truth, having set Perfection as their ultimate goal, choose as their Presence the *Point of Unicity* (the tangible One)—who bears the Essence of the One in its totality—and commune with Him through the divine flux, without any need to envision a particular face. From the *Point of Unicity*, there exists a direct "throughway"—the *metacausal gravitational axis*—that always leads to Perfection. Those who succeed in establishing a connection to this axis, i.e., to *Divine guidance*, and remain steadfast throughout their entire life are quite likely to ultimately reach Perfection.

The *Point of Unicity* is an all-powerful, omniscient, benevolent, and generous entity who looks upon and listens to us each time we direct our attention to Him, and responds to us mostly through our sound reason. The more we have developed our sound reason, the better we can decipher His messages, especially those conveyed through the seemingly minor events of daily life.[12] If we are unable to correctly interpret the messages that we receive, which is generally the case (especially at the

---

11. "Paradise can be envisioned, but Perfection defies all imagination." Ostad Elahi, *Āsār ol-Haqq*, vol. 1, saying 922.

12. "Those who are able to deduce general principles from small details will always thrive, whereas those who draw narrow conclusions from general principles will fare the opposite." (Ostad Elahi, *Paroles de Vérité*, saying 73.) "When we become attentive to the Source, God in turn imparts an 'effect' that enables us to acquire insights from the most minor of experiences, and the particulars of these insights can lead us to glean more general principles." Ibid., saying 153.

outset), we should rest assured that He will bring about what is best for us, both from a material and spiritual standpoint.

In general, if we manage to set aside our preconceptions based on erroneous teachings and representations of God, the soul, and the hereafter—and focus on the *Point of Unicity* or the God of our faith (provided that He is true) or on one of the prophets or saints who are true Essence-bearers, with the sole purpose of coming to know the Truth—we will all behold, upon reaching a level of spiritual development (wherein one sees the Truth as it actually is), the same Truth and the same "Face," regardless of the different cultures, places, or times in which we live. Indeed, once we have acquired the merit to come to see the *Point of Unicity*, He will make Himself known to us by means He deems best, and may even make His "Face" manifest. Until then, it will suffice to focus upon the existence of His Presence, without attributing an imaginary appearance to Him.

Those who concentrate directly on the One, on the *Point of Unicity*, on the true God of their faith, or on one of the prophets or saints that bear the Essence absorb Divine light within their soul. And yet, the metacausal energy emanating from this light is so intense that one would do well to remember that no one has the capacity to bear it. As such, He attenuates this light to the extent that it becomes gentle, pleasant, and profoundly endearing.[13] *Exceptionally, it may come to be that we experience, for a brief instant, an extremely powerful yet gentle, reassuring, soothing, and endearing "luminous" flux emanating from His Presence that extends toward infinity and envelops us and the whole of creation; we sense that we are not alone in praising Him, and that all beings are spontaneously doing*

---

13. "Endearing" in the sense that it gives rise to a feeling of sincere love for the One.

so—all except those endowed with reason who are in a state of total spiritual amnesia; we ardently desire to love and worship Him, and better appreciate that the divine flux is everywhere and in everything, and understand why God is considered the Efficient in all things, while the rest are but causes and means.

Anyone who experiences the tangible presence of His flux, if only once, permanently acquires certitude in the existence of God and the spiritual dimension.

2) *The Dialogue Phase*

Dialogue consists in speaking intimately to the One (the Source of Truth)—by way of the divine flux—in the language of our inner guide. We can begin this dialogue by drawing inspiration from the intimate prayers of the great prophets and authentic divine men and women of the past, especially those that have affectionately invoked His grandeur, generosity, and mercy, and remind us of the duties we must fulfill to draw closer to Him: (1) duties toward ourselves (tending to the overall health of our body and mind, and being diligent in our pursuit of spiritual perfection); (2) duties toward others (being a source of good and beneficence, and helping others to the extent that they can rely upon us); and (3) duties toward the One (directing our attention toward Him, and always striving to align our thoughts, words, and actions in accord with the voice of our conscience and divine contentment).

We should know that during the course of this dialogue, (1) the more our attention is focused, (2) the more our dialogue is centered on Divine generosity and omnipotence, praising and thanking Him for all of the blessings He has bestowed (and continues to bestow) upon us, and (3) the more the mercantile requests of our ego are subdued, the more Divine light our soul will absorb. This does not imply, however, that we will cease to harbor terrestrial-animal desires; rather, they will always remain with us, except for brief and rare moments when our thoughts are absorbed by Him. In general, as long as we are dwelling in our body, we are imprisoned within our ego and remain incapable of fully and wholeheartedly giving preference to divine contentment over that of our own (Figs. 3b and 5). We will always harbor terrestrial-animal desires, whether in relation to our material or spiritual life; in practice, it is enough to keep these desires in check and to refrain from their utterance. If the pressures of material life are more than we can bear, we can always confide in Him and entrust any decision to His grace, without complaining if the outcome is not to our liking. If we address Him with attention, He will always hear our requests, and will respond favorably if what we are seeking is truly in the best interest of our soul. The error lies with us for expecting a quick response that is pleasing to our ego. If He were to respond favorably to all of our requests—which are almost always terrestrial-animal in nature—it would inevitably have a detrimental effect on both our material and spiritual lives. It is best, therefore, to entrust ourselves to His generosity, for He always—through the divine flux—sees our thoughts and hears our inner voice, and will grant us that which is beneficial for our material and spiritual lives, without the need for us to insist upon it.

During this dialogue, we should constantly remind ourselves that the One (or any God that we believe in, provided He is true) is all-powerful, that He is absolutely without need (of us or anyone else), and that He is devoid of any human weakness. We must repeat these three points, especially that He is without need, until they become ingrained in our brain and psyche. Any "god" who is not all-powerful, who is in need of his beings, and who has human weaknesses is not a true God, but rather a fabricated idol borne of human imagination and based on the circumstantial projection of our desires and wishes.

While there may not be much emotional connection during this dialogue at the outset, with perseverance an affinity will gradually emerge in our heart that ultimately transforms into a sincere and lasting love for Him (the rational love of Truth). We must approach Him with humility and see ourselves as small before Him, mindful of the meaning of our words before we utter them. If we are able to express ourselves with heartfelt emotion, it is certain that our message will reach the Source (the One). The more our words are charged with emotion, the more light our soul will absorb and the more we will be drawn to Him. Indeed, when our words stem from the heart, the imperceptible thread that connects us to Him begins to vibrate and we are seized by a distinct and highly appealing emotion. On rare occasions, it may also happen that the words themselves assume life and come into luminous relief as they begin to "speak" . . . Furthermore, His gaze may ignite a spark within us that leads to an ecstatic emotional state (*hāl*)[14] of a metacausal nature, a state

---

14. Even a single "photon" of Divine light can cause our soul to illuminate like a lamp, which brings about a state of "*hāl*"—an ecstatic state of a metacausal nature—or even higher elevated states. *Hāl* is an extremely pleasant spiritual emotion that at times awakens within us a tender sense of nostalgia for the Source, a longing that can bring us to tears, tears that induce joy and euphoria for the soul. Those who are not knowledgeable of the spiritual realm, however, are reminded that negative entities also have the permission and ability to induce—in those who pursue spirituality for the sake of experiencing mystical love and supernatural powers—strong states of *hāl* that are invariably limbic in nature and thus poisonous for the soul. The pursuit of such states makes one easy prey for these negative entities. Yet it is simple to distinguish between the spontaneous metacausal *hāl* originating from the Source of Truth and that which is induced by negative entities. As previously stated, the *hāl* induced by negative entities is

marked by a sense of enchantment, energy, and love for Him, at times accompanied by a tender and enrapturing nostalgia for the Source. We must be careful, however, not to develop an addiction to such states or to actively pursue them, and instead to leave their occurrence to His will.

Humility and Gratitude

As long as we have not allowed the flux of humility and gratitude to flow though our hearts, we cannot experience sincere love for the One. To develop such heartfelt humility and gratitude requires that we remind ourselves of all the blessings that He has bestowed upon us, without expecting anything in return (for He is absolutely without need). The following is a historical example of gratitude as expressed by one of the great saints:

"I was nothing, and You brought me out of 'nothingness' to guide me toward total bliss; it is You who grants life and health; it is You who instills within me the impulse to worship and the impulse to seek truth so that I may have faith in You and seek the Truth; it is You who grants me sound reason capable of understanding Your truths, and the opportunity to apply them to draw closer to You; it is You who grants me all of these material and spiritual blessings, and allows me to benefit from them; it is You who grants good fortune and the joy of life; it is You who is the Efficient in everything—the rest are but means of causality I must negotiate to draw closer to You; You are my only support, lifting me up each time that I fall; help me to see in the hand that lifts me, none other than Yours. Causality in all its truth amounts to nothing

---

always of a causal or limbic nature and thus kindles such terrestrial-animal traits as libido, pride, narcissism, and the will to power, whereas *hāl* of a metacausal nature gives rise to purity, humility, and love for others, while strengthening one's spiritual dimension, in particular one's faith and sincere love for the One. We should recognize that our own imperious self functions as a steadfast ally to such negative entities, serving as both an intermediary and an amplifier.

before You; everything is encompassed in You. Help me to always act in accordance with the voice of my conscience and Your contentment, and to remain sincerely faithful to You; Your contentment is all that I seek; do not allow me to ever commit, desire, or confront anything that is contrary to Your contentment. . . ."

3) *Conditions for the Exercise of Attention-Dialogue*

The conditions for the exercise of attention-dialogue can be summarized as follows:

(a) That we sincerely (wholeheartedly) *seek the Truth, even if our sincerity is reasoned and based on self-persuasion.*

(b) That the Presence we choose (a God, prophet, or saint) and designate as our focal point to engage in a dialogue with the One be true, meaning that it be an actual Essence-bearer so that it can amplify and directly transmit our messages addressed to the One. Here, the Essence-bearer plays the role of an amplifier, bolstering our words and states of being, and directly transmitting them to the Source of Truth (the One). If we choose to focus on the *Point of Unicity*, we should ensure that this Presence bears the Essence of the One in its totality, for Divine light and *living real divine truths* emanate from this Essence for all beings.

If, however, as a result of misleading publicity, fanatic traditional belief systems, blind imitation, etc., we choose as our focal point a presence that is devoid of the Essence (in the mistaken belief that it is true), then no matter how much we focus upon it, we will neither derive Divine light nor any discernment of Truth, much less the ability to reach the Truth. Nonetheless, given that these proselytistic presences are strongly allied with negative entities,[15] they often remain able to induce in their devout followers frequent states of "limbic mystical ecstasy" or *hāl*. As these states of *hāl* are always heavily imbued with pride, narcissism, the will to power, and libido, they inflame the ego of such individuals and fill them with pride and narcissism, without them realizing how they are profoundly poisoning and even impairing their own soul. If a presence devoid of the Essence could in fact lead one to the Truth or to the development of one's sound reason, one would eventually come to realize, after faithfully putting into practice the principles it sets forth as real divine truths, that the presence is false. Yet that is not what we observe.[16] Indeed, without the development of sound reason, it is not possible to recognize *living real divine truths* and to understand that the presence in which we have placed our faith is untrue—i.e., that it lacks the Essence.

(c) That we adopt an attitude of sincerity and humility toward the Presence, for the One is aware of the content of our heart and minds through the divine flux, which envelops and is present in everything. Our sincerity will evoke a response from Him, while

---

15. These negative entities live in symbiosis with our soul and have a similar function to the numerous saprophytic microbes that live in symbiosis with our body. As long as our faith in a true God remains sincere, our spiritual immune system will function properly and these saprophytic negative entities will remain harmless; otherwise, these very entities will become pathogenic for our soul.

16. "Those who are drawn to a false belief or religion—which at its core is devoid of any truth—can never expect their faith to reach a state of certitude." Ostad Elahi, *Āsār ol-Haqq*, vol. 1, saying 99.

our humility will attract His gaze and result in us being heard by Him. By contrast, being arrogant before Him or hardhearted and cruel toward others creates a barrier to the divine flux, which is loath to penetrate a proud and callous heart. The closer we draw to the Source of Truth, the more empathetic, humble, and altruistic we naturally become.

(d) That we strive to purify our intention, to the extent possible, from the terrestrial-animal demands of the ego—even those that assume a "spiritual" guise—and to abide by the voice of our conscience and divine contentment. If we do so, the words that we utter will naturally stem from the voice of our inner guide.[17]

Note that any material or spiritual desire other than seeking divine contentment is considered a desire of the ego. This is the case, for example, when we expect to be rewarded with a state of *hāl* or ecstasy each time we engage in the exercise of attention-dialogue; or expect to develop supernatural powers (clairvoyance, magical healing, wondrous feats, etc.) after a period of practice; or expect immunity for ourselves and our loved ones from illnesses and setbacks in life, etc. These kinds of mercantile expectations stem from the ego, especially the imperious self. If, however, without any prior expectation, we happen to occasionally experience metacausal *hāl* or other states of elation granted by Him, that is positive and is indicative that the One has cast His gaze upon us. The distinction lies in the nature of our expectations and in the Presence that we focus

---

17. The prayers that Ostad has left us, especially the last one, provide a good example. See *Āsār ol-Haqq*, vol. 1, saying 1791; *Words of Faith: Prayers of Ostad Elahi*, ed. Bahram Elahi (Paris: Robert Laffont, 1995), 36.

upon. If our expectations of Him are tainted with mercantile (give and take), terrestrial-animal thoughts, whether related to our material or spiritual life, we risk being deceived not only by our imperious self, but also by negative entities that are constantly seeking to influence and mislead our soul. Conversely, if we solely seek His contentment, not only will He protect us from the deception of our imperious self and negative entities, but He will also grant us that which is beneficial for our material and spiritual lives, without us having to ask for it. Of course, in life, no one is capable of fully and wholeheartedly accepting His contentment in every matter. Yet, He will still credit our effort if we at least try to rationally accept it.[18]

Spiritual Mercantilism

We should avoid, to the extent possible, having a mercantile relationship (give and take) with the One or the God of our faith (if true) and instead assume responsibility for our material lives like everyone else through customary and normal social means, without invoking divine intervention. Indeed, spiritual mercantilism is a disguised ruse of the imperious self. To guard against it, we must bring ourselves (through self-reasoning) not to expect any reward in exchange for our spiritual practice, be it a material reward (success, wealth, power, etc.) or a spiritual one (ecstatic mystical states, clairvoyance, supernatural powers, etc.). Although supernatural phenomena often excite and enchant the

---

18. If the Presence that we concentrate upon is authentic, i.e., an Essence-bearer, it will help us to gradually prefer divine contentment to that of our own. The occurrence of this inner transformation is itself a telling sign that this Presence bears the Essence and has been designated by the Source.

ego, they disrupt one's regular self-consciousness and affect the soul like mind-altering drugs, resulting in dependency. Euphoric states of altered consciousness not only arrest the process of acquiring self-knowledge, but also cause the soul to stray and regress. Under the influence of mind-altering substances, how far can a student (of medicine, for example) expect to advance? By contrast, those who seek divine contentment come to increasingly witness His will in their lives. Such divine intervention is always positive and beneficial, even if displeasing to the ego, and places one's destiny on the right material and spiritual course. Attracting His will in our lives is a fundamental concept: It was the main goal of the true mystics of the past, and remains so for those engaged in the process of spiritual perfection today.

(e) That we strive to sufficiently develop our sound reason in order to correctly interpret His responses. The more we develop our sound reason, the more clearly we can understand His responses and trust our interpretation of them. As such, what was once a one-way monologue becomes a two-way dialogue. Among the many benefits, if not the most important, of drawing upon our sound reason to better interpret the responses that we receive is that it compels us to review, reflect upon, and deepen our understanding of *living real divine truths* archived in our memory. For when divine truths are real and living (as opposed to imaginary or defunct), the very act of reviewing them results in their meaning gradually becoming more palpable to us.

Spirituality in Practice

The exercise of attention-dialogue is but one element of a broader practice of spirituality, which can be summarized as follows:

(1) Cultivating *constant attention* within until it becomes second nature to us, and transforming it into *perfect attention*.[19] Constant attention implies developing the habit of being mindful that the divine flux—imbued with His thought, power, and will—always envelops us, much like the air that we breathe. Perfect attention implies that in addition to having constant attention, we also monitor the ever-harmful activities of our imperious self that are detrimental to our soul. Indeed, if we do not constantly monitor our imperious self, it will surreptitiously divert our attention and substitute falsity for truth in our mind, while reinforcing our pride and egocentrism.

(2) Practicing the exercise of attention-dialogue daily, for a few minutes or more each day.

(3) Applying in daily life *living real divine truths*, including correct divine and ethical principles, in an *in vivo* manner. To do so, we must strive during the course of our lives to always behave in accord with the voice of our conscience and divine contentment.

(4) Fighting ceaselessly against our imperious self. Similar to the process of respiration, which constantly eliminates toxic gases from the body, this struggle must also be constant so as to prevent the "toxic gases" of the imperious self from accumulating in the soul and poisoning it. Those whose souls are poisoned

---

19. See chap. 16.

come to reject outright any notion of God, the soul, and the hereafter. And if they happen to retain their faith in God, they lose all motivation for true divine or ethical acts, or, worse still, become afflicted with an "inverse spiritual outlook" and are drawn to spurious discourse and misguided spiritualities; when confronted with a *living real divine truth*, they look upon it disparagingly and reject it with contempt.

To succeed in our practice, we should remind ourselves that the divine flux always envelops us, and that the Efficient in everything is the One; nothing can come to pass without His will, which always carries a positive and beneficial effect. It fully determines the destiny of all beings and plays a positive role in their lives, except for those endowed with reason and free will. In the case of the latter, He restricts His will so as to allow them to define their own destiny rather than leaving it to divine determinism. As such, human beings, within the bounds of their free will, must chart the course of their own material and spiritual destiny. Nonetheless, the more sincere our faith in the One or in the true God of our faith, the more we will attract His gaze and the more we will come to merit His intervention in our lives and our spiritual destiny. Upon reaching Perfection, our will fuses with that of the One.

If we do not bring ourselves to accept that our own free will plays a determining role in our destiny (material and spiritual alike) until we reach the threshold of Perfection, our outlook on life and the spiritual laws that govern it will be erroneous and will draw us into a vicious cycle of endless protests and objections against God—assuming we have faith in Him—or the ways of the world. For example, when faced with the hardships of life, whether our own or those of others, we cry out:

"If there is a God, why is there so much inequality? Why should all these misfortunes befall me or my loved ones? Why is this happening to me or to them?" etc. Yet because these objections—these whys—are not grounded in correct spiritual principles, they are bound to remain unresolved. With our pride wounded, we sulk and turn away from God, never having understood that due to our own shortcoming, the true cause of our misfortunes lies in our own decisions and actions.

In reality, all those endowed with a sound mind are responsible for their own actions, and whatever befalls them—whether good or bad—is a result of their own doing. By virtue of our free will, we ourselves must account for the wrongs that we knowingly and intentionally commit. During the course of our successive lives on earth, we always appear with the same "self" that is responsible for these wrongs. If these wrongs become numerous in one lifetime, we may have to answer for some of them in our subsequent lives, which partially accounts for the inequalities that are observed in society.[20]

---

20. On this subject, see *Fundamentals*, vol. 4, *Worlds and Interworlds*, chap. 7 (forthcoming).

Chapter 13

The New Medicine of the Soul
Commentary on Figure 6

*This method of battling the ego is like a new
field of medicine intended for the purification
of the soul that I have developed based on my
own personal experience.*[1]

T he new medicine of the soul is a science that is realized through the *in
vivo* practice of *living real divine truths* set forth by *Divine guidance*.
As long as a single rational being remains on any given planet, so too will
Divine guidance be found there. It will be some time yet before human
beings come around and change their views on God, the hereafter, and
spirituality as a whole; in other words, before they consider and realize
that spirituality is a necessity, and must be perceived and approached in
earnest as a formal academic discipline, i.e., as the new medicine of the
soul.

The vast majority of people perceive spirituality as an artform
intended to achieve wondrous acts, supernatural feats, inner peace,
ecstatic spiritual love, and altered states of consciousness rather than as a
science for the sound development of one's thought. Although states of
love, inner peace, and the like are extremely pleasing and attractive to the

---

1. Ostad Elahi, *Paroles de Vérité*, saying 322. "Purification" here refers to the
transformation of character weak points into virtues.

ego, they are ultimately of little benefit to the soul and in all likelihood are actually quite harmful to it. Conversely, the new medicine of the soul, like any experimental science, is not very appealing at the outset, but in the end provides many advantages for the soul. As human beings we have a choice: We can decide to either pursue the art of attaining altered states of consciousness that contribute nothing to our soul, or to pursue the sound development of our thought as a science (i.e., as the new medicine of the soul). The latter will lead our soul to Perfection, whereupon we will forever enjoy a state of total bliss.

The psyche, which we commonly consider to be synonymous with the "self," in fact refers only to a very small part of our real self (our soul) (Figs. 1b and 4). Erroneously limiting our real self to our psyche results in a cognitive flaw in our spiritual thought process and can lead us astray. Our understanding of the psyche and the treatment of its dysfunctions has expanded considerably ever since becoming a formal subject of scientific inquiry. If we approach the understanding of our soul in a similar scientific manner—as the new medicine of the soul—we will no longer feel spiritually bewildered and disoriented, and our futile questions about God, spirituality, and the hereafter will gradually cease.

The new medicine of the soul consists in coming to know our real self, our soul, by way of soundly developing our thought. The human soul is a psychospiritual organism, much like the human body is a biological organism. The relationship between the body and soul is like that of a vessel to its content or a glove to a hand, both sharing a similar organizational and functional structure. For example, like the body, the soul is in possession of sensory faculties (sight, hearing, smell, touch, taste . . .),[2] highly sensitive and subtle emotional faculties, a cognitive and reasoning faculty of great capacity (the metabrain), etc. Consequently, by understanding how our body (biological organism) functions, we can deduce by analogy how our soul (psychospiritual organism) functions and thereby come to better know ourselves and advance our soul with awareness toward its perfection.

The new medicine of the soul, much like the science of medicine, is an experimental science,[3] with the difference that we must first learn to become a physician of our own soul (i.e., come to know our own soul) before becoming a physician that can treat others (i.e., coming to know their souls). Moreover, just as becoming a traditional physician requires connecting oneself (i.e., gaining admission) to an accredited medical school, becoming a physician of one's soul requires connecting to *Divine guidance*. Once such a connection has been established, one must learn

---

2. Like the body, the soul can also lose its sensory faculties, i.e., become blind, deaf, paralyzed, etc. For example, those whose soul is blind or deaf can neither see nor hear the *living real divine truths* they encounter during their life on earth; though their psyche hears, their soul does not and they thus remain unconvinced. Once they return to the interworld, they will fully realize their disability, for in the interworld the Truth becomes manifest.

3. In response to the objection that the new medicine of the soul is a pseudoscience, one should consider that reason, which has the potential to develop like all other human faculties, is capable of grasping ever-deeper dimensions of truth at each level of its development, dimensions that would have been beyond its grasp at earlier stages. Likewise, to grasp the spiritual dimension of life requires the development of one's sound reason, the potential for which exists in all human beings. It would suffice, if only as an experiment, to practice correct divine and ethical principles *in vivo* for a sufficient period of time, whereupon one would realize that the causality and sequentiality that govern in the material dimension equally govern the spiritual dimension. Thus, the designation of a branch of knowledge as a science or pseudoscience is but a function of the scientific progress of a given era. For example, until the laws of chemistry were discovered, some considered chemistry as alchemy or witchcraft.

the *living real divine truths* set forth by *Divine guidance*, apply them in an *in vivo* manner, and successfully pass the corresponding spiritual trials that one must inevitably face. If we content ourselves with generalities and with simply acquiring theoretical knowledge of these truths, without applying them in an *in vivo* manner, we will not be able to grasp them within our deeper self (our soul) and will not acquire self-knowledge (knowledge of our real self). Instead, we will merely add new theoretical information to our intellectual archives.

Furthermore, to become a physician of one's soul, it is essential to adopt the same mindset as that of a student of medicine. However, whereas a medical student needs only his or her common reason to come to know the truths concerning the health of the body and the treatment of its diseases, a student of the new medicine of the soul needs his or her sound reason to discern and come to know truths concerning the health of the soul and the treatment of its character weak points and flaws relating to divine or ethical principles. If such character flaws are left untreated (uncontrolled), they will automatically become pathogenic for the soul and render it weak and incapable: Weak in the sense that one has neither the motivation nor the willpower needed to take on one's spiritual destiny, and incapable in the sense that even if one were to adopt a spiritual practice, one would remain incapable of fighting against these character weak points or flaws, or the imperious self that stems from them.

Those in whom the seed of sound reason has germinated by earnestly adhering to an authentic monotheistic religion, whether in this life or in past lives, are better prepared to engage in the new medicine of the soul. Fortunately, this is the case for the majority of people, even if they currently find themselves in a state of *spiritual amnesia*. What is needed to emerge from this state is a favorable environment that provides them with encouragement and/or a divine glance that awakens their soul and ignites their motivation to pursue spirituality.

As with the study of medicine, the study of the new medicine of the soul entails various academic levels that can be classified into two main stages: the *fundamental stage* and the *advanced stage*. The focus of the fundamental stage is on examining and mending one's faith, sufficiently developing one's sound reason, and cultivating one's humanity, whereas the advanced stage involves delving within one's spiritual unconscious to come to know one's soul and the divine spark (one's quintessential self)[4] that lies within it (Fig. 6). Once we come to know this spark, we will come to know ourselves and to know God within us, and will see that He is everywhere and in everything.

The Fundamental Stage

During this stage, we must begin by examining and mending our faith— that is, by exercising diligence to ensure that we are placing our faith in a true God. Subsequently, by relying on the motivation produced by such faith, we must practice *in vivo* the *living real divine truths* set forth

---

4. The divine spark or *quintessential self* is one's true self, to which even one's celestial soul belongs. "One of the arguments for the existence of the soul is the following: We always speak of '*my* hand,' '*my* leg,' '*my* eye,' and so forth, which implies that this 'self' is separate from all the discrete parts it possesses. Who, then, is this 'self' to which these parts belong? This 'self' is none other than the soul . . . even then, we refer to it as '*my* soul.' What, then, is this 'self' to which even the soul itself belongs?" (Ostad Elahi, *Paroles de Vérité*, saying 176) According to Ostad, this quintessential self appears to correspond to the divine spark borne by the human celestial soul. (*Madjma ol-Kalām*, unpublished manuscript, 38) As long as we do not come to know our quintessential self, which is hidden from us in our spiritual unconscious, we will not be able to fully know ourselves.

by *Divine guidance* to sufficiently develop our sound reason. Drawing upon this faith and our sound reason, we must then seek to cultivate our humanity. With the motivation engendered by our faith, the oversight of our sound reason, and the practice of *living real divine truths*, our regular self-consciousness gradually descends into the depths of our psychological unconscious (Fig. 6). During this journey, our regular self-consciousness relays its perceptions to the brain in order to be analyzed by our sound reason. If our sound reason has not yet sufficiently developed to be able to properly analyze these perceptions, we can turn to *Divine guidance*—which is always present on earth—or consult with those who share our convictions and whose sound reason is more developed. In the more advanced stages, when our sound reason has further developed, our regular self-consciousness also plays the role of a headlamp that enables us to better perceive our character weak points or flaws through the "eyes" of our sound reason.

Our regular self-consciousness must gradually descend into our psychological unconscious while remaining on the *balanced pathway* (Fig. 6)—that is, the pathway that separates the two parts of our psychological unconscious, the terrestrial-animal part and the celestial-human part. In practice, to maintain our regular self-consciousness on the balanced pathway during the descent into our psychological unconscious, we must strive to observe the legitimate rights of our body-id and the legitimate rights of our soul, while also equitably observing the legitimate rights of others.

The following actions, if performed on a regular basis during the normal course of daily life, will automatically guide our descent along the balanced pathway:

- Cultivating *constant attention*[5] within until it is imprinted in our preconscious and becomes second nature to us. Constant attention to God allows us to continuously and gently absorb Divine light in a physiological dose.[6] The amount of metacausal energy that is thus harnessed allows us to develop our faith and our love for God, while keeping our soul and psyche naturally awake (alert) and active. Those who seek to engage in their process of spiritual perfection must also turn their *constant attention* into *perfect attention*—that is, while constantly keeping their attention directed toward God (constant attention), they must at the same time closely monitor the harmful activities of their imperious self in order to identify them as quickly as possible and prevent the imperious self from leading them astray. Indeed, it is through the struggle against the imperious self that we can concretely advance in our process of spiritual perfection. A daily practice that helps cultivate a state of constant attention is to try to always behave (think and act) in accord with the voice of our conscience and divine contentment.

- Practicing the exercise of *attention-dialogue* daily for a few minutes or more; this exercise is also effective in developing constant attention within us.

- Obligating ourselves to practice correct divine and ethical principles—especially beneficence and empathy—in every circumstance and to habitually follow the voice of our

---

5. See chap. 16.
6. "Physiological" in the sense that the amount of Divine light is adapted to the capacity of one's soul and psyche, and therefore does not engender altered states of consciousness that result in the impairment of one's reason.

conscience and divine contentment in our behavior. In addition to developing constant attention, such a practice cultivates our humanity.

- Fighting ceaselessly against our imperious self, this "anti-self" that is the most pernicious, persistent, and harmful enemy of the human soul (our real self). In particular, this struggle requires gradually identifying and taming our character weak points and flaws (relating to divine and ethical principles), from which the imperious self arises.

With time and perseverance, the layer of hazy thoughts (cognitive fog) that envelops the ego will begin to dissipate, the opacity of our psychological veil will diminish, and our connection with our total unconscious (and thereafter with the spiritual dimensions) will expand (Fig. 3a). As a result, the following changes will naturally take place within us over time:

- We will develop a greater sense of empathy and concern for others and will spontaneously seek to come to their aid, especially those who are in need.

- Our spiritual amnesia will decrease, making spirituality an increasingly tangible reality for which we come to develop an affinity.

- The existence of the One or God, the soul, the hereafter, and especially an accounting will gradually become more tangible in our mind, and we will no longer see ourselves as separate from our soul, but rather as one with it. Moreover, we will have no doubt that our lives will continue in the hereafter, and that our quality of life there relates directly to the quality of the development of our thought here.

- We will more quickly and easily recognize the manifestations of the imperious self within us, and will practically come to understand that without the close and steadfast support of the metacausal energy of the One or the God of our faith (provided He is true), we will not be able to overcome the constant attacks of our imperious self, or tame and control our character weak points.

- With the development of our sound reason, the *rational love of Truth* will emerge on the horizon of our thought. This rational love will provide us with a stable and enduring motivation, one that grows with each passing day and enables us to tirelessly persevere and advance toward our ultimate goal—Perfection.

Throughout the fundamental stage in our process of spiritual perfection, it is essential to maintain the regular state of our self-consciousness and avoid entering into any altered states of consciousness. One advantage of descending into our psychological unconscious while preserving the regular state of our self-consciousness is the ability to maintain, without disruption, a normal family and social life.

As our regular self-consciousness descends into our psychological unconscious, which is a reservoir of our character weak points and flaws, we must strive to gradually identify new character weak points that remain hidden from us. In practice, one of the ways of doing so is to remind ourselves of the slate of character weak points and flaws relating to divine or ethical principles and, as we delve further, to look within (analyze ourselves) to see which one of them most demands our attention. We must then assess that weak point in the context of the realities of daily life to confirm our finding. Finally, if our assessment is correct, we must strive to tame and control that weak point.

Another way of identifying our weak points that is accessible to everyone is to become attentive to the words and behavior of others, especially friends and those who are close to us, as they can better see our character weak points. This implies listening to their criticism and analyzing it: if such criticism is correct, we should strive to rectify ourselves accordingly; if it is incorrect, we should dismiss it without harboring any resentment. At the same time, we should also observe the positive qualities and behavior of others and adopt their example: if we do not observe such behavior in ourselves, we should seek to identify the weak point that is preventing us from adopting that behavior. Life in society and our interaction with others provide an invaluable opportunity for identifying our character weak points or flaws. Note that just as we identify an illness of the body through the symptoms it produces, so too can we identify a character weak point through the specific manifestation of the imperious self that it gives rise to within us.

Once we have identified a character weak point or flaw (relating to a divine or ethical principle), our first step should be to attempt to gain control over it at the level of our thought (an *in vitro* practice) through willpower, self-reasoning, and reliance on the metacausal energy of the One, rather than resorting to harsh physical or psychological ascetic practices. We must then proceed to an *in vivo* practice by driving out the imperious self engendered by this weak point—that is, to abstain time and again from carrying out its dictates or even to act to the contrary, until this weak point is eventually tamed. This same approach should also be implemented for each of our other character weak points.

Such an active approach may seem quite difficult at first and we may frequently experience failure, but with perseverance, the process becomes easier and we come to repeatedly gain the upper hand. It should also be noted that this practice takes place within us at an entirely psychological level. Not only does this approach not disrupt the course of our daily life, but it actually contributes to its overall improvement.

Principal Character Weak Points in Human Beings

Each of us can have multiple character weak points and flaws (relating to divine or ethical principles) that must be controlled if we are to advance in spirituality.

The most harmful of these weak points is hardheartedness (a lack of empathy, mercy, and compassion toward others), which shuts off our heart to Divine light (meaning it becomes loath to enter our heart). As a result, we become all the more callous, transgressive, brutal, resentful, and vengeful.

Next is pride and arrogance toward the present Truth. Those afflicted with pride see themselves as superior to others and are thus blinded to their own faults (character weak points), posing a major obstacle to their advancement in the process of spiritual perfection, a necessary part of which is humility. As for arrogance, it leads one to disdain real divine truths, which are often expressed in a language that is simple or at times unconventional.

Thereafter, one can cite a lack of sincerity in spirituality (which renders the soul lame), and beyond that a lack of willpower, lustfulness, and greed. Without willpower, nothing can be accomplished. In reality, most of us possess willpower, for it is essential to our material life and can thus be readily put to use in our spiritual life; the failure to do so is itself a weak point. As for lustfulness and greed, they hinder us from remaining steadfast on any spiritual path, even a true one, causing us to drift from one path to another.

Other prevalent weaknesses include uncontrollable anger; maliciousness; malevolent jealousy; lack of generosity; ingratitude; exclusionary selfishness (wanting anything good solely for oneself); miserliness, or, at the other extreme, unbridled prodigality; malevolence; betrayal and underhandedness; backbiting; lying without justification (that results in harm to others); lust for power and money; lack of fidelity to one's word; lack of common sense . . . On the path of spiritual perfection, a lack of common sense coupled with credulity is extremely perilous, for it renders us vulnerable to thieves of faith and morality: We come to believe everything we are told, regardless of the source, and we mistake imaginary truths for real truths.

For those who have advanced further in their process of spiritual perfection and thus strive to see the Efficient in every occurrence, another weakness is fear of the negative judgment of others, calumny, or defamation.

Aside from hardheartedness, the character weak point most harmful to the soul is lack of faith in a true God. Throughout the course of history, humanity has referred to God by different names. Yet what matters is not the words that are invoked, but the meaning behind them—the unique and peerless God. Given that all true Gods are merged into the One, when we invoke any of the true Gods of history (for example, those of the authentic monotheistic religions), it is as if we have invoked the One. Sincere faith in a true God is essential because it provides the metacausal energy that is required for the struggle against one's imperious self and the formation of divine virtues. A spiritual practice can only succeed if it is sustained by the metacausal energy of the One or of a true God.

The more we come to tame and control our weak points, the deeper we will delve within (our psychological unconscious) and the more we will come to know ourselves; our inner being will become more transparent to us, and we will better interact with the spiritual dimension. In particular, we will be able to better identify the different facets of our imperious self and the character weak points from which they emerge,[7] enabling us to confront them with greater clarity and determination. What is important in the fight against these character weak points and flaws is to persevere—that is, to never let the imperious self out of our sight and to continually maintain the struggle, while entrusting the outcome to the Source.

In the first stages of self-knowledge, the density of the ego's hazy thoughts and the opacity of the psychological veil are such that students of the new medicine of the soul cannot directly perceive or clearly comprehend their character weak points and flaws, nor the faculties that govern their psychological unconscious (Fig. 3b). But as we advance in our self-knowledge and develop our sound reason, these faculties and character weak points become increasingly tangible to us. In addition to coming to know our weaknesses, if we can concurrently come to harness our strengths, we will make a commensurate leap in coming to know our self. These strengths include: (1) greater compassion and empathy toward the misfortune of others, (2) a greater degree of development of one's sound reason, which allows us to better recognize *living real divine truths* and better diagnose and contend with the manifestations of our

---

7. "Once we have engaged in the process of spiritual perfection, we should never lose sight of our ego, which seeks to always mislead us under various guises until our last breath." (Ostad Elahi, *Paroles de Vérité*, saying 66) It is by fighting against our imperious self *in vivo* that we can come to gradually know its different facets.

imperious self, (3) a louder and more effective moral conscience, (4) a higher degree of sincerity and affection toward the One or the true God of one's faith, and (5) stronger willpower, which allows for better control of one's ego. Moreover, if we are also able to (6) acquire certitude that everything is subject to an accounting that no one can avoid, and (7) fully recognize, based on personal experience, that no event or phenomenon in life can come to pass without His approval,[8] we will have made a significant leap in our self-knowledge and can better understand the order within creation established by the One.[9]

Students of the new medicine of the soul who succeed in coming to know their psychological unconscious have completed the first stage in the medicine of the soul (the fundamentals) and acquire the capability (acceptability) to enter the advanced stage. They no longer question the meaning of life, their origin, the reason for their presence on earth, or their ultimate destination. Their humanity, sound reason, and trust in God have sufficiently developed, and their rational love of Truth is strong. Among their most important gains is to have come to grasp the real meaning of the word "God," regardless of their specific culture or faith. An even greater leap is to become aware of the existence of the *Point*

---

8. Those who have reached an advanced level of concrete self-knowledge unanimously affirm that without His approval, we cannot progress in our pursuit of self-knowledge and will inevitably either stagnate or go astray. No one can bypass this principle of spiritual causality. To advance in our process of spiritual perfection, we must always keep in mind that without His approval, the current of causality will come to a halt and nothing can be done or undone: No non-being can come into being, and no being can cease to be.

9. If such order did not reign in creation, no scientific progress would be possible. Scientific discoveries attest to the existence of this order.

of Unicity,[10] which will make everything easier and clearer for them. The *Point of Unicity* is the key that unlocks all the doors leading to Perfection.

The Advanced Stage

After completing the fundamental stage in the process of spiritual perfection, it is wise to dedicate the remainder of our earthly life to further developing our sound reason, increasing our spiritual provisions, and absorbing Divine light. At the same time, as long as we are living on earth, we must earnestly refrain from venturing into our spiritual unconscious—that is, from deliberately crossing the *red line* that marks the border between our psychological unconscious and our spiritual unconscious (Fig. 6). The advanced stage—whose purpose is to acquaint us firsthand with different groups of souls and especially to help us acquire direct knowledge of God within us (the divine spark)—requires crossing this red line into the space (zone) of our spiritual unconscious. Yet it is best that we wait until we are in the interworld before attempting to do so. Though our advancement is more difficult in the interworld, the educational environment is far more favorable, for we no longer find ourselves in the state of spiritual amnesia that grips us here on earth.

The spiritual unconscious is indeed the site of direct contact with souls, of trances, of mystical love and ecstasy, of spiritual feats and wonders. Such states are extremely dangerous for those who are spiritually immature,

---

10. Prior to the appearance of the *Point of Unicity*, those in pursuit of self-knowledge with the goal of reaching Perfection sought to achieve this goal through the God of their faith or the *God of the time* of their own era (the total theophany). Today, those who do not yet know the *Point of Unicity* can still advance toward this goal if they sincerely pursue the true God of their faith or the *God of the time* of a past era (provided the latter was a true Essence-bearer and not an imaginary one.)

which includes virtually all of us. By prematurely venturing into our spiritual unconscious, we will inevitably expose ourselves to strong psychospiritual emotional storms that rob us of our reason and lead us astray. Spiritually immature individuals who, on their own initiative and by means of various psychospiritual techniques (ascetic or meditative practices, etc.), prematurely venture into their spiritual unconscious will necessarily establish direct, and at times tangible, contact with groups of souls,[11] be it negative souls intent on misleading them or positive ones that wish to help them. But it is the negative souls that seek to tempt or mislead us and do us harm that are at the forefront of these groups: They rob us of our reason, induce altered states of consciousness, infuse us with states of limbic mystical love, and confer what are in reality ineffectual pseudospiritual powers upon us (Fig. 6). We will thus find ourselves in a situation like that of an inexperienced youngster surrounded by a gang of dealers who are constantly peddling mind-altering and psychedelic substances. Incapable of distinguishing between the negative entities that want to mislead us and the positive entities that wish to do us good, we are unable to escape from the traps of the former on our own. Those who become ensnared fall prey to intoxicating pseudomystical whirlwinds (limbic mystical love) that sever their connection with the realities of life,

---

11. This type of "contact" is achieved through altered states of consciousness that do not allow one to distinguish between the nature of various souls, some of which are ill-disposed toward human beings. However, should science and technology enable us to tangibly communicate with souls in the future (which will happen) through the use of standard means (for example, by way of images on a screen), such contact will no longer be objectionable for it will not rely upon altered states of consciousness. At that time, all false religions and misguided spiritual paths that cater to the ego will necessarily fall silent, for the Truth will become evident to all through science and technology, and *Divine guidance* will become accessible to everyone and easy to follow for the majority.

inevitably leading them astray. Unless rescued by the *Point of Unicity*, some go as far as to experience psychosis and/or delirious states that are at times characterized by megalomania.

Exceptionally, it may happen, by the will of the *Point of Unicity* and under His direct protection, that we are led into our spiritual unconscious during our lifetime and safely ushered past the danger zone with our "eyes and ears covered,"[12] in which case we will reach our metabrain and come to grasp everything through it: We will recall our past lives and become aware of our *quintessential self*, the divine spark to which our soul belongs. We will thus come to know this divine spark within our soul (i.e., we will come to know ourselves) and will come to tangibly know the true God within us. We will then see that God is everywhere and in everything, and will realize that it is within ourselves that we should have sought him all along, for the distance separating us from Him is a perceptual one, not a spatial one.

Throughout this process, the germ of *becoming annihilated in God*,[13] which exists in the soul of all humans, blossoms and overflows our being with divine passion; all fear subsides, giving way to true metacausal love, as we desire nothing but to unite with Him. It should be noted, however, that as long as we have not reached the stage of perfect love,[14] our soul is not entirely free of its responsibility to its physical body and id (its

---

12. "Eyes and ears covered" in the sense that as long as we dwell within our body, we remain seemingly unaware of the spiritual states we are ushered through, even as we benefit from the positive effects of these states on our psychological unconscious. For example, we develop an inner certitude in the existence of God, and nothing can erase that certitude.

13. See chap. 2, note 10.

14. "When you become ready to receive His love, love will come." Ostad Elahi, *Āsār ol-Haqq*, vol. 2, 262.

body-id); thus, we are not at liberty to irreparably endanger, on our own initiative, the health or life of our body, even if it is for a higher cause. That is also why the new medicine of the soul advises against all forms of harsh ascetic practices for the body-id.

At this point, three more stages still remain to reach Perfection. The completion of these three final stages requires such a degree of metacausal energy that it can only be granted by the One. By virtue of this energy, our love for the One (the rational love of Truth) reaches its apex, our mature sound reason is transmuted into divine reason by the One, and our entire being becomes a certifying conscience: Like a drop of pure water, we acquire the acceptability to merge with the Ocean of Truth (Perfection). There, commensurate with the capacity and station of our soul, we will forever live with complete awareness in one of the levels of Perfection, overflowing with metacausal love for the One, in total bliss.[15]

"Souls that have reached Perfection enter a realm in which everything is subject to their dominion and experience a state that defies all description."[16]

---

15. "Anyone who puts forth the effort will reach one's own level in Perfection. God grants one who reaches even the lowest level of Perfection all the ecstatic states that exist in creation . . . states that never repeat themselves or lose their freshness, each more exhilarating than the last. The quality of such ecstatic states is experienced equally by everyone: the difference at the higher levels lies solely in the extent of one's understanding of that which is Divine. . . ." Ibid., 284.

16. Ostad Elahi, *Paroles de Vérité*, saying 87.

Chapter 14

The Inner Conflict, the Imperious Self, Self-Mastery, Natural Spirituality
Commentary on Figure 7

> *This path . . . is not one of words, but of deeds; only through action can progress be realized.*[1]

T his chapter will address the following topics in turn:

1) *The inner conflict*: A conflict that results from the instinctive opposition between the faculties of the terrestrial-animal part of our psychological unconscious and those of its celestial-human part, manifesting at the level of our conscious self in the form of an inner dialogue between our ego and our inner guide;

2) *The imperious self*: An extremely powerful psychological energy that continuously emanates from our psychological unconscious and is harmful for the soul, leading us to systematically think and act contrary to societal laws and correct divine and ethical principles;

3) *Self-mastery*: The total mastery of our ego by our inner guide; and

---

1. Ostad Elahi, *Paroles de Vérité*, saying 6.

4) *Natural spirituality*: A form of spirituality that is actively practiced in the midst of society and through interaction with others, one that observes the legitimate natural rights of both our body-id and our soul while avoiding any altered states of consciousness.

1) The Inner Conflict

The inner conflict results from the constant, instinctive confrontation between the faculties of the terrestrial-animal part (the tandem of the id and imperious self) of our psychological unconscious and those of its celestial-human part (the superego). The purpose of this inner conflict is to give rise to a flux of cognitive thought within our psyche pertaining to God and ethics.

The Inner Dialogue

The inner conflict manifests at the level of one's conscious self as an inner dialogue between the ego and the inner guide. By way of example, the ego confronts the inner guide as follows: "Life is short, let me be so I can enjoy its pleasures to the hilt! Who has ever definitively proven that God, the soul, the other world, and an accounting exist, and that life continues beyond death? Who in their right mind leaves cash on the table for a promise of future credit? Why do you insist on imposing your stringent divine and ethical rules, which make no sense to me and only sap my pleasure?" The inner guide retorts: "Be quiet and listen to me! You're acting like a primate—your understanding is limited to that of a small child who only cares about having fun and instant pleasures. You live in the present and are incapable of anticipating the future. You have no understanding of the value of ethics and spirituality, for you

---

cannot grasp the Transcendent. . . . Besides, who has ever definitively proven that God, the soul, the other world, and an accounting do *not* exist, and that we will *not* continue our life in the other world after death? The fact is, you're my complement, and we need one another. It's my duty to tame you and to take you under my tutelage. If I succeed, we will rapidly advance in unison toward Perfection and a state of total bliss."

There is a significant difference, however, between the opposing forces within our psychological unconscious: Terrestrial-animal thoughts are produced naturally and abundantly by the tandem of the id and imperious self, as well as our common reason, such that they are strongly felt ("heard") at the level of our ego, whereas celestial-human thoughts produced by the four faculties or consciences of our superego (the certifying, inspiring, and blaming consciences, together with the superid), as well as our sound reason, are only faintly felt ("heard") at the level of our inner guide. To feel these celestial-human thoughts more strongly and to better analyze ourselves, we need to strengthen our inner guide by soundly developing our thought. In reality, like light that overpowers darkness, the energy that arises from our superego and manifests through the inner guide is far more effective and incisive than that which arises from the tandem of the id and imperious self. Yet, as long as we are present in our physical body, we feel ("hear") terrestrial-animal thoughts far more acutely. The goal of pursuing the sound development of our thought is to reverse the current of our thoughts to the benefit of our superego so that we can feel ("hear") more effectively the thoughts that emanate from our inner guide.

Without soundly developing our thought, we will not develop our sound reason and thus will be unable to strengthen our inner guide. Consequently, we will automatically be subjugated by the terrestrial-animal thoughts of the ego and our thoughts will become dominated by the imperious self, which unfortunately is the case for virtually all of us. Those who dismiss or neglect ethics and spirituality outright will not strengthen and make more audible the voice of their inner guide. The clamor of the terrestrial-animal faculties that constantly arises from their ego will eventually drown, or even completely stifle, the voices of the celestial-human faculties that arise from their inner guide (Figs. 4 and 7). Acting contrary to divine and ethical principles will no longer engender any remorse within them, and whatever concern they may have had for their spiritual destiny will also gradually disappear. Their thought will become saturated with the wants and desires of their ego and common reason, and they will no longer be subject to any restraint based on divine or ethical principles. Whatever faith they may have maintained will eventually fade and they are gradually led astray. Ultimately, with the passage of time they transform themselves, to varying degrees, into a kind of humanoid primate enslaved by the pursuit of pleasure. Outwardly they are human in every respect and may even be perceived favorably by others, yet internally they are governed by an animal endowed with an intelligence that is directed toward deceitful and noxious ends. In other words, despite their often well-groomed appearance or pleasant disposition, inwardly they nonetheless remain devoid of humanity and any divine or moral constraints. Extremely selfish and with no compassion for others, they think only of their own interests and are solely concerned with pursuing the self-centered pleasures of their ego. Deception and lying have become second nature to them. Fortunately, those who believe in the God of their religion, or in the soul and life beyond physical death (especially an accounting), or who have encountered and were drawn to a correct ethical and spiritual education during their childhood and youth (or in a past life), have a minimum of sound reason that enables them to more or less keep themselves in check and avoid plunging into such an abyss.

2) The Imperious Self

The imperious self is an extremely powerful and spiritually harmful psychological energy that continuously arises from the psychological unconscious of all individuals endowed with reason and discernment,[2] manifesting at the level of the conscious self. Within our psyche, it can be considered an "anti-self" that systematically opposes us as soon as we (i.e., our inner guide) make a decision to apply a correct divine or ethical principle and/or place our faith in a true God; conversely, this same "anti-self" encourages us when we decide to renounce our faith or act contrary to a correct divine or ethical principle. The imperious self is specific to human beings who, unlike animals, are endowed with reason and discernment. Given that animals lack reason and a moral sense, they are unable to distinguish good from evil or legitimate from illegitimate; rather, they are guided by their instincts, and as such do not generate the imperious self.

The imperious self at times manifests in our conscious self in the form of emotional thoughts (pressing impulses and desires), and at times

---

2. What is meant here by "discernment" is the ability to discern right from wrong.

in the form of deceitful rationalizing thoughts;[3] most often, however, it expresses itself as a mixture of both. Although contrary to correct divine and ethical principles, these impulses and desires are generally pleasant—extremely pleasant, in fact—for our ego, though they can also be unpleasant or even painful, as is the case, for instance, with envy and greed, pessimistic ruminations, depressive or suicidal ideations, and rancorous or jealous thoughts (especially toward loved ones and acquaintances).

In general, the impulses and desires of our imperious self do not respect divine and ethical limits; instead, they continuously prod our psyche to reject beliefs and prescriptions based on correct divine and ethical principles, and to embrace their contrary. For example, based on correct divine and ethical principles, our inner guide strongly encourages us to believe in God, to avoid transgressing the rights of others, to be empathetic, to not seek revenge and to forgive, etc., whereas our imperious self pushes our psyche to do the opposite—to solely think about ourselves and to seek nothing but our own selfish pleasure.

Just as we eliminate toxic gases from our lungs through the continuous process of respiration, so too must we continuously wage a battle against our imperious self in order to expel "spiritually toxic gases" from our "spiritual lungs." For if we do not expel these gases from our thoughts or neutralize them, they will gradually poison our psyche and from

---

3. Deceitful in the sense that such thoughts lead us to devise justifications for illegal, anti-divine, or unethical actions, as we deceive ourselves into believing that such acts are indeed not harmful for our soul and may even be beneficial for our psyche (for example, they will prevent us from developing a psychological complex). In reality, resisting anti-divine and unethical impulses and desires with the intention of advancing in our spiritual perfection does not create a complex, regardless of any pressure exerted on our psyche.

there our soul, and can even undermine our judgment. A prominent sign of those whose souls are poisoned is that they not only lack any motivation for the practice of true spirituality and correct ethics, but their perception of the Truth and real divine truths is inversed, meaning they consider real truths as falsehoods and falsehoods as real truths. For instance, the deceitful words and writings of religious or spiritual merchants and swindlers invoke their admiration, while the words and writings of authentic spiritual figures automatically provoke their criticism and denigration. As a general rule, they tend not to believe in God or in the hereafter, and if they were to believe in a god, it would be in one that solely advocates for them, a robotic god that is programmed according to the desires and thoughts of their ego and of those who share their convictions.

The imperious self imposes its impulses and desires at times by force, at times by deception, and, should we mount any resistance, by way of recurring temptations. In rare instances, it may also induce a chronic excess of spiritual scruples in individuals who are exacting and hypersensitive in matters of spirituality.

(a) With regard to force: The imperious self rebels[4] by hijacking our reason and willpower, forcefully imposing its desires and compelling us to robotically obey its commands. During such attacks, we are solely concerned with satisfying the desires of our imperious self, without considering for a moment the repercussions of our negative acts from an ethical or spiritual standpoint; and if we were to feel a pang of guilty conscience, it

---

4. "To 'rebel' means that it transgresses [divine and ethical] limits and becomes defiant." Ostad Elahi, *Borhān ol-Haqq*, 564.

would always be after the fact. In reality, because our reason and willpower are under the control of our imperious self, we are no longer able to resist its desires, even as we are aware that the act we are committing is contrary to correct divine and ethical principles. When the imperious self rebels, its flames can only be extinguished by a burst of metacausal energy from the One. At that point, the only remedy is to sincerely solicit the help of the One, or of the *Point of Unicity*.

(b) With regard to deception: The imperious self infiltrates our common reason by concealing itself behind pleasing yet tainted and toxic justifications to deceive us. For example, at the outset, we fool ourselves into thinking that we are superior to others, and attribute blame to them for our own actions and thoughts that are counter to correct divine and ethical principles. At the next stage, the imperious self makes our impulses and desires appear so legitimate as to make us think to ourselves: "Everyone else is doing it, so why shouldn't I?" Or, if we abstain from certain acts for fear of divine punishment, we may think: "Since others are doing these things and nothing untoward is happening to them as a warning, then there is no problem and I can do the same." At the final stage, under the pretext of modernity, freedom, and open-mindedness, the imperious self can even go as far as to deceive us into believing that its desires and whims are generally permissible, if not beneficial, ultimately leading us to disregard *all* divine and moral boundaries. In general, the greatest deception of the imperious self is that it strengthens our pride and superioritism, thereby concealing from us our own character weak points and flaws relating to divine or ethical principles.

(c) With regard to recurring temptations: With incessant tenacity and tireless perseverance, the imperious self overwhelms us with repeated temptations until we capitulate and it succeeds in imposing its desires upon us.

(d) With regard to the chronic excess of spiritual scruples: In rare cases, the imperious self may engender a chronic and uncontrollable excess of spiritual scruples in certain individuals who are exacting and hypersensitive in relation to their ethical and spiritual duties. Thus, each time they prepare to engage in an action related to spirituality or divine and ethical principles, their chronic excessive scruples bring them to doubt themselves and wonder: "Have I made the best choice?" or "Does God approve of my choice?" This quality is generally more prevalent among women.

3) Self-Mastery

Self-mastery refers to the total mastery of the ego by the inner guide. Such mastery is achieved when—under the direction of our sound reason, and through reliance upon strong willpower and the steadfast support of the metacausal energy of the One—we are able to impose the directives of our inner guide upon our ego and acquire complete control over the ego's faculties. In practice, this process involves gradually coming to know within us the character weak points or flaws (relating to divine or ethical principles) from which the imperious self arises, confronting each of them in an *in vivo* manner, and persevering in this struggle until we are able to completely tame and control them. At this stage, however, mastery has yet to be achieved. Mastery of a weak point only becomes permanent and part of our being after the One has cast His gaze (*divine touch*) and transmuted that weak point into a divine virtue, thus becoming part of our soul's genetic makeup.

Psychological Virtues and Divine Virtues

We can choose to develop two kinds of virtues within us: purely psychological virtues or divine virtues. To develop a purely psychological virtue, there is no need for faith or belief in God; this type of virtue can be developed through rigorous mental disciplines or harsh physical or psychological ascetic practices. However, because these virtues are not assimilated by the soul, they disappear upon physical death. Divine virtues, on the other hand, require faith in a true God and can only be developed with the metacausal energy of the One. By His will, these virtues become permanently inscribed in the soul and do not leave us upon physical death. Integrated into the genetic makeup of the soul, a divine virtue remains with us wherever we are, whether in this world during the course of our successive lives or in the hereafter. Although they appear similar on the surface, a divine virtue is a means to achieve divine contentment, whereas a purely psychological virtue is a means to derive personal pleasure or to impress others.

We will not be able to achieve self-mastery (mastery of the ego) by way of our inner guide if we do not complement the active struggle against our character weak points and flaws with an effort to control our id. That is because the id (our pure animal nature) is not only at the genesis of our character weak points, but also serves as their reservoir. Given that we know the imperious self arises from the activity of our character weak points, it is imperative that we control our id to prevent our character traits—which have a natural tendency to lapse into excess and stray—from transforming into new character weak points. Controlling the id implies taming and controlling the animal character traits that stem purely from our terrestrial soul. To do so, we must respect the legitimate desires of the id while being mindful they do not lapse into excess or stray so as to form new character weak points. For example, when we are hungry, we can enjoy the food of our choice, but without eating in excess, while avoiding those foods that are harmful to our body. Similarly, we must provide our body and psyche with healthy forms of recreation to prevent weariness, but avoid at all cost any form of recreation that risks irreparable harm to our body or psyche.

Without an *in vivo*[5] struggle against our imperious self that is closely supported by the metacausal energy of the One, self-mastery is all but impossible. In practice, this struggle involves a direct confrontation between our inner guide and our imperious self (Fig. 7). The confrontation against the temptations of the imperious self can be likened to that which takes place in a videogame: With every strike against the imperious self, our inner guide earns a point and we further advance toward our spiritual perfection. It is on the stage of the "game" of life that our inner guide must remain vigilant as we journey toward our spiritual perfection, for as long as we lack complete mastery over our ego, our imperious self

---

5. The battle against the imperious self must take place in an *in vivo* manner—that is, in concrete, real-life situations. For example, a jealous person must fight against this flaw in relation to those he is jealous of, or a person who backbites must fight against this flaw in relation to those he is prone to backbite or with whom he participates in doing so.

(adversary) will always recover from every strike and resume its attack. Unlike the virtual characters in a videogame, however, the inner guide and the imperious self are two actual mental personas that govern our psyche and play a decisive role in our spiritual destiny.

To achieve the desired outcome in our struggle against the imperious self, we must connect ourselves to *Divine guidance*, develop and strengthen the requisite willpower to fight, and recharge ourselves spiritually, especially through positive readings, or, better yet, through the regular exchange of ideas—whenever possible—with those who share a common goal.

Our inner guide has the following weapons at its disposal: (1) sincere faith in a true God (which enables us to receive the metacausal energy of the One, without which the ongoing struggle against the imperious self, and thereby the process of spiritual perfection, becomes impossible); (2) sound reason (which, if sufficiently developed, can recognize the imperious self and lead the fight against it);[6] (3) a well-trained moral conscience (which sounds the alarm); (4) the impulse to worship (which gives us faith and the energy for practice); (5) the rational love of Truth (which results in steadfastness and perseverance); (6) strong willpower (which imposes the directives of our inner guide upon our ego); and (7) the metacausal energy of the One (which is the only energy that can neutralize the powerful and spiritually harmful energy of the imperious self within us).

In practice, the *in vivo* struggle against our imperious self must be carried out on four fronts:

---

6. Until such time as we reach Perfection, we are always in need of the close help and counsel of a strong sound reason.

- First front: We must strive to drive out and neutralize the pressing impulses and desires of the imperious self as soon as we detect them in the space of our conscious self. It is important to note that the struggle against the imperious self requires perseverance and persistence. Like a boxer fighting a strong yet deceptive and tenacious opponent, we must constantly be on guard to neutralize the ruses of our imperious self, repelling and forcefully quashing its arguments and coercions. When it comes to the persuasions of our imperious self, we should avoid engaging in reasoning, for in doing so our defeat is all but certain. If our attempts to ignore it are not enough, which is generally the case, we must fend off its attacks with the "counterpunches" of our willpower and with support from the metacausal energy of the One. Whenever we can, we must also seek to do the opposite of what these impulses and desires dictate. For example, if an unwarranted negative or immoral thought regarding a person or persons crosses our mind, we should firmly drive it out with our willpower and replace it with positive thoughts, and whenever possible, compel ourselves to act to the contrary. If the imperious self resists and becomes increasingly coercive, we must immediately seek help from the *Point of Unicity*, whether His identity is known to us or not; the simple act of invoking Him, provided that we do so with sincerity (from the depths of our heart), is enough for us to receive help.

Given that one of the characteristics of the imperious self is its obstinate persistence, we too must be persistent in our struggle against it. Whenever we drive the imperious self out of our mind, it immediately returns time and again; thus, we too must drive it out time and again. We must persist in this struggle until a combative mindset against our imperious self becomes second nature to us and we even come to develop a taste for it. To avoid becoming discouraged, we must recognize that what counts, especially in the beginning of our spiritual journey, is to never leave the "ring" and to continue fighting, no matter how often we face defeat. What matters at the outset is to persevere and not give in.

- Second front: By relying on our faith in the One or in a true God, and with the help of the metacausal energy of the One, we must strive to tame and control our character weak points and flaws, which act as a factory that generates the imperious self within us. When a character weak point reaches functional equilibrium in this manner, it acquires the potentiality to be transmuted into a *divine virtue* through the *divine touch* (divine gaze). Only a sincere faith in the One, or in the God of one's religion (provided He is true), brings about the metacausal energy necessary to transmute a character weak point into a divine virtue. Such divine virtues are among the constant factors that contribute to the soul's immunity against the toxins of the imperious self; they automatically produce the neutralizing antitoxins to the character weak points that give rise to them. For example, those who possess the divine virtue of compassion are naturally loath to be hardhearted and maleficent. They are genuinely sensitive to the suffering of others, which they seek to alleviate as much as possible.

We should keep in mind that when we seek to fight against and tame a character weak point, it usually rebels and counterattacks with an outburst, like a spitting snake: in other words, the desire associated with the weak point we are fighting suddenly intensifies. That is why when confronted with such a situation, we must be vigilant and strive to repel and neutralize the poisonous outburst of our character weak point with the help of the metacausal energy of the One. If our own efforts prove to be insufficient, we should ask for help, whether from the One or from the *Point of Unicity*.

- Third front: We must fight against the recurring (chronic) temptations of our imperious self. In the face of recurring temptations, we must stand firm and neutralize them each time they flare up. Some of these temptations may stay with us until the end of our lives, but if we continue fighting them—even if we do not succeed in fully neutralizing them—they will not hinder our progress toward spiritual perfection. Indeed, the very act of fighting our imperious self will automatically result in our advancement.

- Fourth front: If one is affected by a chronic excess of spiritual scruples, the only remedy is to consult an experienced and trustworthy advisor and, for a period of time, apply to the letter what that advisor recommends on this subject. If we are unable to find such an advisor, but continue our struggle while placing our hope in Divine generosity, He will see to it that this condition does not hinder our spiritual progress. As such, an excess of spiritual scruples, though upsetting to our psyche, will not prevent our soul from advancing in its process of spiritual perfection.

In summary, the imperious self can be likened to an inherently despotic and delinquent "anti-self" that is cunning and obstinate. It will not relent until our last breath, unless we were to succeed in fully mastering our ego. In the battle against our imperious self, what matters is to not remain neutral and passive, but instead to be vigilant, persistent, and perseverant. Even though we fail more often than not (especially at the outset), the mere fact of persisting in our struggle will help us to advance, and the end result we attain will exceed our expectations. Although the imperious self always holds the upper hand in the beginning, we must not allow these repeated setbacks to discourage us. By persevering in this struggle, as our sound reason develops (and, in proportion, our rational love of Truth), so too does our resolve and motivation to overcome the imperious self. Thereafter, the tides slowly and gradually begin to turn, and we are the ones who increasingly come to gain the upper hand.

It would be wrong to assume that if, on a single occasion, we manage to fend off or neutralize the imperious self generated by one of our character weak points (especially a causal charge),[7] the matter will be over and done with. Indeed, we may face that same weak point hundreds, if not thousands, of times over, until our efforts reach a point where we come to merit having it transmuted into a divine virtue by the One. This same process applies to our other character weak points as well.

---

7. For more on causal charges, see chap. 11.

4) Natural Spirituality

To achieve mastery of the ego, the spiritual path that is most reliable and at the same time most compatible with an active and productive life in society is that of *natural spirituality*. "Natural" implies that those who engage in their process of spiritual perfection with the goal of reaching Perfection must strive in the course of their practice to observe the legitimate rights of their soul and the natural rights of their body-id, as well as the legitimate rights of others; "natural" also implies that everything one perceives and learns in the realm of spirituality must be through one's *regular self-consciousness* (the natural or normal state of one's consciousness) as opposed to altered states of consciousness. The following three points should therefore be kept in mind:

(a) As the "body" (body-id) and the soul both have legitimate rights, we must equitably observe the legitimate rights of each in its own place. The "body-id" refers to the ensemble formed by the physical body and the id (the pure animal nature in the human psyche), which manifests in our conscious self at the level of our ego, just as the soul manifests in our conscious self at the level of our inner guide.

The relationship of the physical body and the id to the soul is like that of two legs or a pair of mutually indispensable collaborators.[8] The soul has a duty to watch over and control

---

8. "We must tend to our body out of a sense of duty rather than passion, and turn our passion instead to the strengthening of our soul. The body [body-id] functions as a pair of legs for the soul, without which we could not reach our destination. Thus, we must always strive to maintain an equilibrium between the body and the soul." Ostad Elahi, *Paroles de Vérité*, saying 245.

them by means of its sound reason so that they do not lapse into excess (to either extreme) and stray; as such, in the hereafter (where we will all appear in the form of our subtle body), it is the soul (our real self) that will be deemed responsible and held to account, not the body-id. Those who undertake their process of spiritual perfection must equitably observe the legitimate rights of their body-id as well as those of their soul,[9] recognizing that the soul can also lapse into excess and stray through the activity of the four consciences of the superego (the certifying, inspiring, and blaming consciences, and the superid).

The legitimate rights of the body-id require that we tend to the health and integrity of our physical body and fulfill the legitimate needs of our id,[10] while neither repressing the body-id and stifling its instincts through self-mortification,[11] as do the ascetics, nor becoming enslaved to these instincts by completely abandoning the reins of our thought to the imperious self, as is

---

9. If there is a conflict between their legitimate rights, the soul takes precedence. "For example, given that altruism is a way of strengthening the soul, it takes precedence over the rights of the body. However, the soul only takes precedence over the body as long as no fatal risk is posed to the latter." Ostad Elahi, *Āsār ol-Haqq*, vol. 1, saying 512.

10. We must never voluntarily expose ourselves to potentially irreparable physical harm—often meant to induce a rush of adrenaline—for the extreme thrill of the ego.

11. Stifling the instincts of the body-id by means of severe physical ascetic practices such that the ego can no longer generate the imperious self amounts to releasing the soul from all the bonds of the ego and abandoning it to the whirlwinds of altered states of consciousness. Once the ascetic practice is discontinued and the body has regained its strength, one's character weak points become ever more active and generate an imperious self that is even more virulent, whereas the soul has grown weaker.

the case with spiritual amnesiacs (which includes virtually all of us). We must therefore tend to our physical body and our id while gradually controlling our ego and bringing it under the tutelage of our inner guide. A spiritual practice that leads to self-knowledge (knowledge of one's soul) and from there to Perfection through the sound development of one's thought necessarily rests upon the close and active cooperation between the body-id and the soul. Repressing and stifling the legitimate instincts of the body-id by imposing harsh ascetic deprivations, whether physical or psychological in nature, is akin to paralyzing our soul by depriving it of the use of its "two legs."

(b) At every stage in the process of spiritual perfection, we must preserve our regular (normal) state of self-consciousness and stay clear of any altered states of consciousness. That is because such states impair our reason and inevitably mislead and distance us from the goal (Perfection). Those who engage in their process of spiritual perfection with the aim of reaching Perfection must process everything they learn in the realm of spirituality through the channel of their regular self-consciousness and sound reason, and not through an altered state of consciousness. Therein lies the main distinction between natural spirituality and other forms of spirituality that pursue love, mystical ecstasy, and supernatural powers (clairvoyance, divination, etc.), or lull one's mind into intermittent periods of "dormant states" through various meditative techniques[12] and altered states of

---

12. Yoga, meditation, hypnosis, psychotherapy, etc., when used solely with the intention of improving physical health, increasing concentration, reducing stress, or as a substitute for anxiolytics or antidepressants, can be positive and beneficial

consciousness.

(c) Finally, we must strictly observe the legitimate rights of all beings, especially those of our fellow beings.

---

for the body and psyche. Yet it should be noted that they are not substitutes for one's spiritual work, for they do not develop one's sound reason.

Chapter 15

The Sound Development of Thought
Commentary on Figure 8

Without the perfection of thought, the perfection of the soul cannot come to be.[1]

The development of our soul parallels the development of our sound reason: The more our sound reason develops, the more our soul develops. Although the essence of the soul is unknowable, it is possible to interact with the soul by way of our thought so as to educate and "nourish" it through the practice of correct divine and ethical principles.

Our thought originates from our soul (our real self), which continuously imbues our brain and psyche with thoughts of a rational and/or emotional nature. After interacting with the environment, these thoughts return back to the psyche, and from there to the soul, influencing them in turn. The circulation of thought in the soul and the psyche is comparable to the circulation of blood within the body: Just as nutrients that enter the blood spread throughout the body, spiritual nutrients absorbed by our thought spread throughout the psyche (the mind), and from there the soul. Thus, it is by virtue of the *sound development of one's thought* that we can nourish our soul and develop it toward its Perfection.

---

1. Anvar, *Malak Jan Nemati*, 114.

The sound development of one's thought entails the *in vivo* practice of *living real divine truths* until they have been assimilated by the psyche, and from there by the soul. It should be noted that the sole energy that can enable these truths to be assimilated by the soul is the metacausal energy of the One, which is specifically harnessed through the practice of constant attention (attention to the omnipresence of the divine flux). The sound development of one's thought is a spiritual educational process that requires parallel work on two complementary fronts, the "thought front" and the "action front."

- **The Thought Front** (*in vitro* practice): On the thought front, we must come to learn *living real divine truths* and, in parallel, cleanse our psyche of "refuse" thoughts—those that are contrary to correct divine and ethical principles, especially unwarranted and tainted thoughts regarding others. To cleanse our thought, we must envision that the One, by way of the divine flux, is always omnipresent and observant. Turning within, we must reproach ourselves, our soul, whose very substance is dignity: "It's beneath your dignity to allow such unwarranted and tainted thoughts to pollute you knowing that He is looking upon you. Remember that the law of action-reaction dictates that others will think and speak ill of you! If you dislike others harboring such thoughts about you, then don't foment such thoughts yourself and expel them from your mind." To clear our mind of such thoughts, no amount of willpower is sufficient and we require the steadfast support of the metacausal energy of the One (which is harnessed through the practice of constant attention). And even if on occasion we were to succeed in doing so, we would quickly tire and give up, leaving the imperious self unfettered to continue polluting our thoughts, and from there, our soul. In addition, the very effort of cleansing our thought is an important factor in developing constant attention. Constant attention not only enables our soul to absorb the metacausal energy of the One in a continuous manner and at a physiological dose, but also allows us to remain resolute and steadfast in our effort to cleanse our mind and psyche of "refuse" thoughts.

- **The Action Front** (*in vivo* practice): On the action front, we must seek to connect our thought to *Divine guidance* and apply in an *in vivo* manner the *living real divine truths* set forth by this guidance, while concurrently developing our constant attention into perfect attention, which entails having constant attention not only to God's presence, but also to the activities of our imperious self.

Conditions for the Sound Development of Thought

To correctly pursue the sound development of one's thought, we should strive to observe the following conditions: (1) to seek the Truth with sincerity and to set Perfection as our ultimate goal, (2) to engage in self-reflection until we come to recognize and acknowledge that we are truly in a state of spiritual amnesia, (3) to engage in an *in vivo* practice, (4) to adopt the right comportment in action and not just words, and (5) to exercise patience.

(1) The first condition for soundly developing one's thought is to *seek the Truth with sincerity and to set Perfection as our ultimate*

goal. Those who set Perfection as their ultimate goal consider spirituality to be an experimental science, comparable to the science of medicine. And like a student of medicine, they must follow the appropriate causal sequential steps to obtain a "doctorate" (self-knowledge) and from there a "professorship" (Perfection). But if they settle for generalities and approximations instead of sufficiently developing their sound reason through the *in vivo* practice of *living real divine truths*, they will end up getting mired in philosophical sophistry and rhetoric and will not reach their ultimate goal. Perfection of the soul is realized when, as a result of the sound development of one's thought, we have completed our knowledge of *living real divine truths*, developed our sound reason to its maturity, and acquired the acceptability for our sound reason to be transmuted into divine reason by the One.

(2) The second condition for soundly developing one's thought is to *engage in self-reflection until we come to recognize and acknowledge that we are truly in a state of spiritual amnesia.* Doing so will make us vigilant to not give full credence to our spiritual thoughts at face value without having first undertaken the necessary diligence. If we properly engage in self-reflection, we will come to realize that we do not know ourselves, meaning that we do not know who we are or what constitutes our real self. If our real self is our soul and a hereafter exists, then why are we here in this world? What is our *essential duty* here? Where do we go after death, and what will our situation be in the hereafter? To find the right answers to these questions, we must begin

by accepting, by way of self-suggestion, the following basic principles as functional hypotheses:

- o The One (the original God), the soul, the hereafter, and an accounting exist;

- o Our real self is our soul, and the purpose of our presence on earth in this human body is to complete the fundamental stage in our process of spiritual perfection, which essentially consists in examining and mending our faith (i.e., exercising diligence to ensure that our faith is placed in a true God), sufficiently developing our sound reason, and cultivating our humanity;

- o Upon leaving our body, we will continue our life in the hereafter, a world that is adapted to the nature of our soul. What is important to note is that life in the hereafter, as in this world, abides by the foundational principles of gravitation, opposites, causality, legitimate rights, connection, etc., and that the quality of our future life there is directly related to the quality of thought that we have cultivated here. If we do not accomplish anything spiritually positive for ourselves here, the foundational principle of causality implies that we will be left empty-handed and remorseful there, and may even have to resort to "mendicity";[2]

- o Within our psyche (overall mental space) are two opposing

---

2. That which is to be earned must be earned here in this world; in the other world, we either reap the fruits of our labor or must resort to mendicity. Anvar, *Malak Jan Nemati*, 133.

"personalities" that coexist in perpetual confrontation: the voice of our ego (the spokesperson for our terrestrial-animal nature), which drives us by force or deception toward the unbridled pursuit of pleasure, and the voice of our inner guide (the spokesperson for our celestial-human nature), which encourages us to adopt a divine and ethical comportment. This spontaneous opposition between the ego and the inner guide results in an inner dialogue[3] at the level of our conscious self (Fig. 7). We should strive to bring ourselves to carefully listen to this dialogue and to implement the advice of our inner guide. For example, we should heed the voice of our conscience, which stems from our blaming conscience, and follow through on the impulses to worship and to seek truth stemming from our superid: The impulse to worship awakens faith in God within us, while the impulse to seek truth leads us to seek and apply *living real divine truths* in an *in vivo* manner.

(3) The third condition for soundly developing one's thought is to *engage in an* in vivo *practice:* that is, to apply in an *in vivo* manner the *living real divine truths* set forth by *Divine guidance* in order to gradually grasp within our being, and acquire certitude about, the veracity of the basic principles accepted at the outset as functional hypotheses leading to reality (the existence of the One, the soul, the hereafter, and an accounting). It is only through such an *in vivo* practice that we can come to concretely

---

3. For more on the nature of this inner dialogue, see chap. 14.

recognize the manifestations of the imperious self within us and to understand that the imperious self is the single biggest obstacle to the sound development of our thought, and that we can neither repel nor neutralize the imperious self without support from the metacausal energy of the One. In the battle against the imperious self, we must exercise strong willpower and perseverance, without allowing ourselves to be discouraged by repeated setbacks, for our imperious self will accompany us and remain active until our last breath. As such, we must always keep the "engine"[4] of our soul running through the practice of constant attention, while boosting its "power" and "speed" with the help of the daily exercise of attention-dialogue (for a few minutes or more each day).

(4) The fourth condition for soundly developing one's thought is to *adopt the right comportment*, meaning to carry ourselves as a true human being in action rather than just words. This comportment involves both our thoughts (intentions) and our actions: We contemplate a given action, make a firm decision to do it (intention), and then carry out that decision (action); collectively, these steps define our comportment. To adopt the right comportment, we must listen to the voice of our conscience in our daily lives and observe the rules and prescriptions intended to ensure order and peace in society as set forth by wise governance. The golden rule is to put ourselves in the place of others, doing unto them that which we want and do for ourselves, while that which we avoid and consider as

---

4. See chap. 17.

harmful for ourselves, we likewise deem harmful for others and shield them from it to the extent possible.

For the voice of our conscience (the blaming or moral conscience) to advise us correctly, it must be trained with correct divine and ethical principles, those that originate from the Source and not from the imagination of our fellow beings. Without such training, the blaming conscience cannot be deemed entirely reliable: it risks raising its voice when it should otherwise remain silent, and to paradoxically remain silent when it should be raising its voice or even shouting. By contrast, for those who have benefited from a correct education based on divine and ethical principles, heeding the voice of their conscience is akin to acting in accord with divine contentment, even if they do not have faith in God as set forth by the religions. However, it should be said that without faith, morality alone often falls short in the face of the strong temptations of the imperious self.

(5) The fifth condition for soundly developing one's thought is to *exercise patience* until we have sufficiently advanced in our process of spiritual perfection so as to come to develop a sustained affinity for it. As the journey along this path is long, we should not allow ourselves to become discouraged and impatient, wondering why despite the many years of effort and struggle against our imperious self, we have failed to reach our desired goal sooner. Indeed, the sound development of our thought requires years, even lifetimes, of practice before we can reach our ultimate goal (Perfection). However, during this process

many positive changes nonetheless begin to take place within us, such as a greater affinity for the practice of true ethics, an enduring peace of mind and inner serenity, and a more humane, compassionate, and empathetic disposition toward others. The changes thus acquired become inscribed in our soul and remain with us, positively and significantly influencing the quality of our life in this world and in the hereafter. When we sufficiently develop our sound reason, an enduring, rational love of Truth appears within us and our patience for the process of spiritual perfection will automatically grow; we may even develop a sustained affinity and appreciation for it.

For those starting out in their process of spiritual perfection, this initial step of developing and "self-imposing" the habit of practicing the principles that lead to a sound development of thought is among the most challenging, for it puts one's patience to the test. But if we sufficiently persevere along this path, we will gradually obtain the following tangible results: The state of *perfect attention* will crystalize in our preconscious— eventually becoming second nature to us—and lead to the development of our sound reason. In turn, the development of our sound reason will enable us to better diagnose the manifestations of our imperious self[5] and to better learn how to dispel them from our mind and neutralize them; with experience, we will be able to grasp the positive effects of metacausal energy on our ability to neutralize the imperious self; we will come to better understand the essential meaning of sound reason and the

---

5. In general, until we have sufficiently developed our sound reason, we are incapable of immunizing our soul against the harm induced by our character weak points and imperious self.

rational love of Truth; and our own love for spirituality and the One will grow stronger. These tangible results will automatically guide us to adopt the right comportment and, more importantly, will increase our desire and motivation to pursue our spiritual journey.

Finally, one should be reminded that engaging in the process of spiritual perfection is an inward matter based on rationality—the rationality of our sound reason. This process is one in which peculiar and eccentric conduct has no place, whether in action or in words. On the contrary, it is an internal process characterized by natural, dignified, and sensible behavior. Those who are involved in this process remain active in their family and social life, and do not in any way grandstand or hold themselves out as superior to others. They carry themselves with humanity and kindness, and are beneficent. They respect the legitimate rights of others, striving to never transgress them.

The Impact of a Sound Development of Thought on the Evolution of the Conscious Self

The conscious self, which is formed mainly by the ego and the inner guide, is a mirror of our soul (inner self)—it reflects all of our psychospiritual faculties. Once we have sufficiently developed our sound reason through the proper development of our thought, we can access it to peer into the mirror of our conscious self and assess ourselves: Do we sincerely believe in God, the soul, the other world, and an accounting, or do we consider them to be empty myths? And if we do believe in them, do we care enough to put forth the effort to research and deepen our understanding of them? (Fig. 8)

In the mental space of our conscious self, the ego and the inner guide have an inverse relationship such that when one is strengthened, the other is weakened. If we do not strengthen our inner guide with the help of *perfect attention* and the *in vivo* practice of *living real divine truths*, our ego will automatically dominate the entire mental space of our conscious self, and the impulses and desires of the imperious self will assume control of virtually all our thoughts.

We will now examine the evolving states of our conscious self throughout the course of life.

1) *The Conscious Self of Newborns* (Fig. 8a)

The conscious self of newborns has yet to take shape: they live within the conscious self of their previous life, while their present life is directed by the instinctive intelligence of their id.

2) *The Conscious Self of Adults* (Fig. 8b)

As adults, we experience life through our reduced self and are thus in a state of spiritual amnesia; this amnesia can be more or less advanced, and in some cases even total (Fig. 3b). Its main cause is the opacification of the psychological veil, which separates to varying degrees the conscious self from the total unconscious, the latter being directly responsible for our communication with the spiritual realm. Our ego occupies a major part of our conscious self and imposes terrestrial-animal thoughts upon our psyche. For the majority of us, *our present thoughts are of a terrestrial-animal nature and are dominated by our imperious self*. From time to time, as a result of an encounter with a spiritual figure, an echo arising from our inner guide, or some other occurrence, we are reminded of God and the world beyond, and come to worry about our spiritual destiny. If we do not heed and follow through on these moments, these echoes will gradually weaken within us and our interest in true ethics and spirituality will wane, as we allow ourselves to be swayed instead by the prevailing social currents of the time. From a spiritual standpoint, if we fail to act, we will eventually become completely subjugated by our imperious self, which will take control of our psyche and govern us according to its wishes; not only will we not resist its desires, but we will chase after them instead (Fig. 7).

3) *The Conscious Self of Those Who Are Subjugated By Their Imperious Self* (Fig. 8c)

Those who are subjugated by their imperious self are in a state of total spiritual amnesia (Fig. 6).[6] Like a chick in its shell, the conscious self of such individuals is enclosed in an opaque layer formed by the hazy thoughts (cognitive fog) of the ego and the psychological veil (Fig. 3b). The opaque and obscure thoughts emanating from their id and imperious self completely dominate their conscious self, and the voice of their conscience is extremely weak, if not inaudible. As the development of their sound reason is blocked, they analyze and manage their lives through their common reason, which is at the service of the tandem of their id and imperious self.[7] Given that their spiritual amnesia is total,

---

6. The types of individuals presented in Figs. 8c and 8d represent extreme cases. In reality, the majority of people are spiritually situated along a spectrum between these two extremes.

7. The cognitive fog emanating from a psyche saturated with the imperious self is so dense and obscure that *living real divine truths* cannot penetrate it. Thus, even if such individuals adhere to a given religion, they will interpret its commandments and prescriptions through their emotions and common reason, which are at the service of the tandem of their id and imperious self. As such, they will make decisions based on the contentment of this tandem (their ego) instead of the

they consider as real only that which relates to their physical self and the material world. Their sole preoccupation is to satisfy their libido and will to power, or, in other words, their selfish desires and whims of a terrestrial-animal nature, especially those of their imperious self. They are impervious to such notions as God, the soul, life after death, etc. They find the idea of an accounting in the hereafter to be ridiculous, a product of human imagination meant for the naive and feeble-minded in search of psychological comfort. Inwardly, they reject all limits relating to divine or ethical principles that stand in the way of their desires, and instead adhere to a self-proclaimed morality that allows them to justify all manner of behavior. They are generally hardhearted and merciless, and transgress the rights of others at the first real or perceived opportunity without any remorse; they exude pride and conceit. Duplicity, mendacity, manipulation, and contrivance have become second nature to them, such that they deceive even themselves and believe they are flawless and superior to others.

Among those who are subjugated by their imperious self, there are some who are driven by social circumstances, cultural or tribal pressures, or the fashion of the day to adhere to a religion (with or without a god), an outdated spirituality, a philosophical school of thought, or a code of ethics devised by those who echo their own thinking. In reality, the choice of a religion, spirituality, philosophy, or ethics for these individuals is led by the tandem of their id and imperious self, which has their common reason at its service. Their main goal is to acquire power, gain recognition, affiliate with a group, or forge a network. If they happen to believe in a "god," their imagined god must, like a preprogrammed

---

voice of their conscience and divine contentment.

robot, comply with the wishes of their ego or the desires of the group. They mold their ethical principles such that they do not stand in the way of the desires of their id and imperious self. And if they happen to believe in a hereafter for the sake of attaining paradise, theirs is a "paradise of the ego," especially one intended to elate the imperious self.

4) *The Conscious Self of Those Who Are Spiritually Awakened* (Fig. 8d)

A spiritually awakened person is one who is automatically in search of the Truth. Such individuals have raised their head out from the shell of their reduced self and have greater communication with their total unconscious; they do not doubt the existence of God. Their sound reason is well-developed and their inner guide occupies the greater part of their conscious self, thereby allowing them to see and evaluate themselves to an extent in the mirror of their conscious self. As a result, the ability of their ego—especially their imperious self—to pressure their psyche is reduced. They easily discern *living real divine truths* from imaginary or defunct truths; they have no weakness for ephemeral values, nor are they lured by futile pursuits (whether of a material or spiritual nature). Given that they are sincerely seeking the Truth, the One will guide them—wherever they may live or whatever their culture—and will not allow them to be duped by the staged theatrics and deceptive words of misguided spiritual paths, "soulless" religions, and godless philosophical ideologies.

Parallel to their spiritual life, they lead an active material life that is productive for themselves and their loved ones, as well as for society as a whole. They earn their own livelihood so as not to be in need of or dependent upon others, and are thus able to think freely. They do not perceive any separation between their material life and their spiritual life, considering them instead as two complementary domains, for they recognize that it is only within the framework of an active and financially secure life in society—in interaction with others—that they can practice correct ethical principles in an *in vivo* manner and thereby cultivate their humanity.

They align their behavior in accord with the voice of their conscience and divine contentment. As a result, a state of constant attention gradually develops within them that ultimately becomes second nature. Thereafter, they do not feel alone or abandoned in any situation. They are convinced, through the experiences of daily life, that the One is the Efficient in everything, and that without His approval, no one can either help or harm them. And should they experience an unpleasant event, they know that the ultimate outcome will definitely be to their benefit; they consider such events as spiritual lessons coming from Him, as a means to remedy the psyche and soul, or as a way to avert the occurrence of graver events.

Divine Assistance (God's Helping Hand)

People often have a mistaken perception of divine assistance. They imagine that His intervention and assistance must be immediate, direct, and overt, while circumventing causality. In particular, they expect such intervention to result in some immediate and tangible improvement in their material situation, emotional well-being, and social life. They overlook the principle of causality, according to which God does not do anything for human beings endowed with reason (aside from rare exceptions) without taking into account their merit or going through the relevant causal channels. This implies that we must first acquire the merit to receive His aid and do our utmost to address our concerns through conventional and lawful means before we can hope that God will resolve them indirectly through other people or material means.

If we have sufficiently developed our sound reason and are attentive, we will be able to perceive His help—which is abundant and occurs at every moment—in the details of our daily lives. In addition, we should be mindful that the fulfillment of some of our wishes is not in our best interest, something that we will likely come to realize in time. That is why we should entrust the result of our actions to God and avoid complaining, even if the result is not to our liking.

Those who are spiritually awakened consider their true reality to be their soul (a psychospiritual organism) and their physical body (a biological organism) to be a means for their soul's process of perfection. The continuation of life in the hereafter and the existence of an accounting have become tangible realities. They are in control of their id (pure animal nature) so that it does not lapse into excess and stray, and actively fight against even the faintest manifestation of the imperious self. In their relations, they put themselves in the place of others and, to the extent possible, want and do for them all that they deem good and beneficial for themselves. They behave with humanity and kindness; they are quite forgiving and stay true to their word. They have a tender and compassionate heart, and enjoy helping others and sharing in their sorrows. They exhibit a peaceful and gentle nature, and do their utmost to avoid any rancor or revenge.

They are quite exacting when it comes to the observance of rights, especially the rights of others. They avoid transgressing the legitimate rights of others (within the bounds of their spiritual understanding), but defend their own legitimate rights when necessary. To observe the legitimate rights of their body-id, they strive to maintain its health physically and holistically, while providing their id with legitimate forms of recreation. To observe the right of their faculty of reason, they cultivate it through the study of pragmatic subjects, whether material or spiritual. To observe the right of their willpower, they avoid any form of dependency that can weaken it. And to observe the right of their soul, they fight against their imperious self, diligently pursue the sound development of their thought, engage in the daily exercise of attention-dialogue, etc.[8]

As their sound reason develops, the rational love of Truth increases within them: In addition to providing a strong and stable motivation to pursue their process of spiritual perfection, this love engenders within them an enduring state of serenity and felicity, coupled with a sense of security and contentment. They have come to know the unique Truth that lies behind "the One" or "God," and how to draw closer to it. They are optimistic and filled with hope for the future. They do not fear death, for they are certain that they (their soul) will never die, and that death is but a change from one dimension to a higher one. They know that to die is to shed this heavy, dark, stifling, and cumbersome physical body— in which virtually all of us subsist in a state of spiritual amnesia—and to enter a new world, where one will continue to live with the same

---

8. "Life, maturity, willpower, reason, dignity, knowledge, rank and station, virtue, and piety have been entrusted to us by God. To breach one's duty toward any of them is a betrayal of that trust: To neglect one's health is to betray life; to be capricious is to betray maturity; to lack resolve is to betray willpower; to be narrow-minded is to betray reason; to be base is to betray dignity; to remain ignorant is to betray knowledge; to abuse one's power is to betray one's rank and station; to engage in debauchery is to betray virtue; to live impiously is to betray piety. . . ." Ostad Elahi, *Borhān ol-Haqq*, 13.

sense of self in the form of a subtle body, a transparent and weightless replica of the physical body. This new world (the interworld) is similar to our earthly world, only far vaster, more beautiful, and more luminous, where an atmosphere of peace, joy, and hope prevails; it is a world where mendacity and duplicity, calumny and aggression have no place, where the reality of each person is manifest, and where none can transgress the rights of another.

As long as they are living on earth, they may nonetheless at times be overcome by the fear of death due to human nature. But these bouts of fear are short-lived, and they are quickly able to rid their minds of it. At the same time, they recognize the value of material life in its rightful place; they are serious and active in society, for they are aware that it is only in this earthly school that one can complete the fundamental stage in the process of spiritual perfection.

As we have seen, the completion of the fundamental stage requires that we: (1) examine and mend our faith—that is, to exercise diligence to ensure that the God in which we are placing our faith is a true God; (2) develop our sound reason by being attentive to the One (the Source of Truth) and practicing *living real divine truths* in an *in vivo* manner; and (3) cultivate our humanity with the help of our faith and sound reason. Toward that end, we must gradually unearth our humanity, buried beneath the thick layers of our animal self, and cleanse our psyche over time of its egoistic and aggressive animal tendencies, replacing them with humanity, kindness, and altruism.

Once we have completed the fundamental stage in this world, we will acquire the acceptability to remain in the interworld—a world that is superior to this earthly one in every respect—to pursue and possibly complete within its "learning institutions" the advanced stage in our process of spiritual perfection in order to reach Perfection.

Chapter 16

Constant Attention and Perfect Attention

What is essential in spirituality is to have
perfect attention to the Source.[1]

Human beings endowed with reason have a duty to turn their attention toward God in order for Him to look upon them. In both his oral and written teachings, Ostad places great emphasis on *constant attention*, though in practice his ultimate aim was *perfect attention*. Whereas constant attention is directed solely toward the omnipresence of God, perfect attention is simultaneously directed toward the omnipresence of God and the constant presence of the ever-harmful activities of our imperious self for our soul.

Constant Attention

Constant attention is to be mindful that the divine flux is always omnipresent and envelops us, and that any good that befalls us stems from the One, while any evil that befalls us stems from our imperious self. As long as we maintain this state of mind, He will never leave us alone and without support, abandoned to our own devices.

The development of constant attention requires working on both our thoughts and our actions. The work on our thoughts entails striving to

---

1. Ostad Elahi, *Āsār ol-Haqq*, vol. 1, saying 2.

remind ourselves on a daily basis (and as often as possible) that the divine flux, like the air that we breathe, is ever-present and constantly surrounds us;[2] thus, the One is able to see and hear our thoughts at every moment. The work on our actions, which is the more important aspect, entails striving in daily life to act in accord with the voice of our conscience and divine contentment, especially toward others. If we persevere in such behavior, over time a state of constant attention will crystalize in our preconscious[3] and will become second nature to us. Thereafter, each time we turn our attention toward the One, we will feel that the divine flux envelops us and that we are not alone. Of course, *the divine flux always envelops us; what is important is to remind ourselves that He always encompasses us and is ever-present and observant.*[4]

Accordingly, the practice of constant attention mostly manifests in a comportment that is in accord with the voice of our conscience and divine contentment. This practice does not imply withdrawing from an active family and social life and retreating to some corner to engage in

———————————

2. Returning to the analogy between the body and the soul, it could be said that just as we breathe pure air when we want to oxygenate our body, so too must we direct our thought toward the divine flux that always envelops us if we wish to "oxygenate" our soul. Each time we concentrate upon the presence of the divine flux, our soul "breathes" in an amount of metacausal energy and is thereby "oxygenated."

3. What is intended by the preconscious is a narrow zone of consciousness situated between the conscious self and the psychological unconscious. The preconscious is a reservoir of thoughts we are not yet aware of, but which remains accessible to our mind. As soon as we turn our attention to such thoughts, they immediately enter our conscious self (Fig. 7).

4. "Considering Him 'present and observant' should be understood in a literal sense—that is, in every circumstance we should consider Him to be both present and observant of all that we do. . . . Of course, God is always present and observant; it is up to us to make ourselves aware that He is present and observant." Ostad Elahi, *Paroles de Vérité*, saying 381.

repeated incantations of God or formulaic mantras, to partake in lengthy meditations on the supernatural, to immerse ourselves in euphoric altered states of consciousness, or to empty our minds for prolonged periods through mental exercises, etc. While such techniques and practices may temporarily soothe our psyche, engender *hāl* of a limbic nature,[5] or induce states of zen, they are hardly beneficial to the process of spiritual perfection for they do not contribute to the development of our sound reason; on the contrary, they result in dependency and the stagnation, if not regression, of one's process of spiritual perfection.

Perfect Attention

Perfect attention consists in having simultaneous attention to God and to the harmful activities of our imperious self. Whereas the practice of constant attention solely increases our love for God and engenders *hāl* of a metacausal (non-limbic) nature, the practice of perfect attention not only engenders a love for God that is balanced, but also develops our sound reason, facilitating and accelerating its development toward its perfection (divine reason).

Those who have set Perfection as their spiritual goal must strive to transform their constant attention into perfect attention: Just as we use our willpower to try and consider God omnipresent and observant of our thoughts and actions, so too must we simultaneously keep an eye on the activities of our imperious self, until this practice becomes second nature to us. We should recall that the imperious self is a powerful psychological energy that is harmful to the soul, yet generally appealing to the psyche. This energy, produced instinctively and continuously in

5. See chap. 12, note 14.

the psychological unconscious of all human beings who have reached the age of discernment, spontaneously occupies our conscious self. The imperious self constantly pressures our psyche to engage in anti-divine and unethical thoughts and actions in order to stop and/or divert our progress toward spiritual perfection. Given that this pressure on our psyche is constant, our attention to the harmful activities of our imperious self must likewise be constant.

The advantage of perfect attention is that (a) our attention to God (constant attention) enables us to harness the metacausal energy necessary to keep our soul alive and active, and (b) our attention to the harmful activities of our imperious self enables us to more readily recognize its manifestations. Thereafter, with the help of the metacausal energy of the One, we can more effectively fight against the temptations of our imperious self in an *in vivo* manner and more effectively neutralize them, thereby developing our sound reason more rapidly. Thus, for those who are engaged in their process of spiritual perfection, it is essential that they transform their constant attention into perfect attention, for the sooner they can diagnose the manifestations of their imperious self, the easier they can neutralize them and the faster they can develop their sound reason and advance toward Perfection. Perfection is realized when a mature sound reason is transmuted into divine reason by the One.

Chapter 17

Journey Toward the Origin

The [human] celestial soul comes directly from God, without any intermediary.[1]

Our real self, our very being, is our soul. The process of spiritual perfection refers to the process by which our soul returns to its primordial Origin, whereupon it forever lives in total bliss. If we are here on earth and separated from our primordial Origin, it is for the purpose of completing the fundamental stage in our process of spiritual perfection. If we do not make a sufficient effort during our initial sojourn here on earth to complete this fundamental stage—which is almost always the case—we (our soul) will be sent back to earth (for a limited number of times) and endowed with a new physical body.

Those who are committed to engaging in the process of spiritual perfection to rejoin their primordial Origin can be likened to a driver in a vehicle traveling on an unfamiliar and mountainous road, one that is icy, winding, and exceedingly long. It is a journey fraught with "thieves of faith";[2] without the assistance of *Divine guidance*, it is impossible to set

---

1. Ostad Elahi, *Paroles de Vérité*, saying 365.
2. "Thieves of faith" refers to leaders and missionaries of strayed spiritual paths, anti-God philosophical movements, new religions, etc., who issue prescriptions that are pleasing to the ego. These thieves are supported by negative entities that by nature are opposed to the advancement of the human soul and are authorized to infiltrate the imperious self and lead astray those individuals who seek spirituality

out alone on this road without losing one's way. Moreover, given that their time is limited, they must hurry if they are to reach their destination.[3] Seated behind the wheel of this "vehicle," they must not see themselves as being alone; rather, they must imagine that seated next to them is this invisible but potent Essence-bearing *Presence* that is always ready to come to their aid.

Here, the vehicle symbolizes our soul (our real self); the driver symbolizes our conscious self; the ignition symbolizes our attention to the Source of Truth (*constant attention*); the steering wheel symbolizes our free will; the Presence symbolizes for some the *Point of Unicity*, and for others the God of their faith or one of the great Essence-bearing saints; the fuel symbolizes the energy-producing metacausal substance that is acquired through the *in vivo* practice of *living real divine truths* and the daily exercise of attention-dialogue; the long mountainous road symbolizes the journey toward spiritual perfection; the roadmap or GPS[4] symbolizes *Divine guidance*; the gravitational force that keeps the tires of the vehicle in contact with the ground symbolizes our id (our pure animal nature), whose instinct of survival binds us to earthly life and allows our soul to remain here and to draw upon life in society so that we can undertake the fundamental stage in our process of spiritual perfection; and finally, the force that impedes the advancement and acceleration

---

as a means to inner peace, ecstatic mystical love, supernatural phenomena, etc., or who pursue a false religion to profit materially and receive the backing of a given community.

3. "In order to reach Perfection, one must keep the goal in mind and race toward it without pause or distraction. In such a state of mind, the true traveler is unaffected by the slow pace or fatigue or other impediments along the way." Ostad Elahi, *Paroles de Vérité*, saying 413.

4. Without the sound development of one's thought, the roadmap or GPS naturally remains inaccessible to us.

of the vehicle toward its goal, constantly working to stop or veer it off course, symbolizes our imperious self.

Those who are engaged in their process of spiritual perfection keep the "engine" of their soul running through the practice of constant attention, set their soul in motion through the *in vivo* practice of *living real divine truths* set forth by *Divine guidance*, and increase the "power" and "speed" of their soul through the daily exercise of attention-dialogue for a few minutes or more each day. But from a practical standpoint, how does one come to realize a state of constant attention? By always trying, to the extent possible, to remind ourselves during the activities of daily life of the constant presence of the divine flux, while at the same time aligning our behavior with the voice of our conscience and divine contentment. The more our thoughts and comportment are in accord with the voice of our conscience and divine contentment, the purer the fuel we obtain, the more speed our vehicle (our soul) accumulates, and the less we risk stalling or veering off course.

Our conscious self—primarily a combination of our ego and our inner guide—is the driver of this vehicle. By virtue of our free will, we can steer the wheel in the direction of our choosing. The direction that we choose depends upon the nature of the impulses and desires that dominate our thought at any given moment: If our thought is dominated by terrestrial-animal impulses and desires, it is our ego that will assume the wheel and the tandem of the id and imperious self will dictate our choice. In such a case, it is quite likely, if not certain, that the imperious self will seize the wheel and veer us off course. By contrast, if our thought is dominated by celestial-human impulses and desires, it is our inner guide that will assume the wheel and our sound reason—relying upon the *Presence*—will lead us directly toward the ultimate goal (our Origin).

During our daily lives, whenever we focus our attention on our thoughts, we can easily recognize the kind of impulses and desires that are dominant within us at any given moment. If it is the impulses and desires of the imperious self that dominate, we can rectify our thoughts and align them with the wavelength of our inner guide with the help of our willpower and support from the metacausal energy of the One (harnessed through the practice of constant attention). At times, however, the imperious self rebels—that is, its pressure on our psyche becomes so great that it exceeds our ability to neutralize it. In such cases, we must immediately focus on the Presence that we have envisioned beside us and sincerely ask for His help in order to expel the imperious self from our thoughts or neutralize it. Without support from the metacausal energy of the One, which comes to us from that Presence, no one can withstand the pressing and recurring impulses and desires of the imperious self, and it is all but certain that we will veer off course.

To benefit from the support of the metacausal energy of the One, the Presence that we envision beside us must be true—i.e., it must bear the Essence so as to be directly connected to the One—in which case the impact will be immediate and our imperious self will be neutralized. But if this presence is not true—i.e., if it lacks the Essence—then no positive outcome will ensue. In fact, therein lies a key spiritual test to assess the authenticity of the Presence we are focusing upon and from whom we are seeking help against the attacks of our imperious self: Only if the Presence is an Essence-bearer can we obtain a positive result; a presence that is not true (devoid of the Essence) wields no power against the imperious self.[5]

---

5. Those who follow a "presence" that is devoid of the Essence (i.e., untrue) face a great danger: If their faith in this presence is solely for material purposes, it is

Given that we have set Perfection as our ultimate goal, we envision a Presence by our side whenever we seek to have attention. Yet until we actually focus our attention on that Presence and request His help with humility and sincerity, it would be counter to divine justice for Him to preferentially come to our aid instead of another. The One dictates the destiny of all beings devoid of reason, but to avoid defining the destiny of those endowed with reason and free will, He attenuates His will to a level that is commensurate with theirs. By virtue of our reason and free will, until such time as we have reached Perfection, we ourselves are responsible for our own destiny, be it material or spiritual. It is thus incumbent upon us, through our thoughts and actions, to attract His gaze so that He may be further involved in our choices and our destiny. A natural and reliable way to do so is to develop a state of constant attention until it becomes second nature to us, such that the "engine" of our soul is always running, meaning that we are always spiritually awake and active.

Divine intervention is always of a positive and salutary nature—all the good that befalls us stems from Him. The more we align our thoughts and behavior with the voice of our conscience and divine contentment, the more we will benefit from His positive effect on our lives, advancing with greater speed and less peril toward our primordial Origin. And each

---

possible that God may draw upon the force of this faith to "miraculously" grant their wishes and thus reinforce their faith in this false presence. The error here lies with the followers in seeking God for the sake of fulfilling their material interests. Indeed, those whose faith and hope is based on the resolution of their material concerns (such as financial issues or physical ailments) may at times witness these "miracles," regardless of whether the object of their faith is a person, a manmade statue, a sacred site, etc. That is why the One cautions us against the spiritual danger of seeking God and spirituality for our material benefit. See Ostad Elahi, *Paroles de Vérité*, saying 253.

time we stray from our spiritual course due to the imperious self—which occurs countless times—He steers us back. That is why for true divine figures, His contentment has always held precedence over that of their ego.

The journey toward spiritual perfection (the return to our primordial Origin) is extremely long and replete with thieves of faith intent on luring us and leading us astray. To undertake such a journey, we are in absolute need of *Divine guidance* and help, strong motivation and willpower, and a great deal of patience. The challenge lies at the outset of the journey in terms of connecting ourselves to *Divine guidance*. Without such a connection and the steadfast support of the *Point of Unicity* (the tangible One), no one can reach the ultimate destination (Perfection). The practice of constant attention keeps the soul—and thereby our faith—active and alert,[6] while faith motivates us and strengthens our willpower. When it comes to patience, however, we ourselves must cultivate it by sufficiently developing our sound reason until the rational love of Truth emerges within us. This rational love of Truth spontaneously brings about patience and motivation; thereafter, under the influence of this rational love, we naturally develop an affinity for the Truth and for *living real divine truths*, and continue the remainder of our journey with patience and motivation.

As for those who remain totally indifferent to their spiritual destiny during their lives and do not commit to engaging in their process of spiritual perfection—that is, they do not keep the "engine" of their soul running through the practice of constant attention and do not provide

---

6. A sincere faith in the One or in a true God is a sign of a soul that is awake and vigilant. Those with an awakened soul are spontaneously drawn toward true spirituality and ethics.

their "vehicle" with the necessary fuel through the *in vivo* practice of *living real divine truths*—how can they possibly undertake the journey toward Perfection and rejoin their Origin? According to the foundational principles of gravitation and acceptability, as long as we have not acquired the requisite acceptability—i.e., as long as we have not aligned the gravitational force of our soul with that of the Source of Truth (the One)—we cannot unite with the Source (the universe of Perfection); the latter will not accept us. By contrast, if we commit to diligently work toward our spiritual perfection by aligning our thought and comportment with the voice of our conscience and divine contentment, while concurrently leading an active and productive life that benefits us, our family, and society at large, then the rational love of Truth will gradually emerge within us. Driven by the motivation engendered by this rational love of Truth (a love that stems from our sound reason), we will thereafter advance directly toward our Origin. In particular, seeking divine contentment has the following consequences:

1) The Presence at our side shields us from thieves of faith and helps us not to come to a stop, fall asleep behind the wheel, or permanently veer off course. And should we inadvertently make a mistake, which is all but certain, He will come to our aid and steer us back on course; and

2) The One (the Creator) connects us to *Divine guidance* by way of our thought, and provides us with earnest travel companions[7]

---

7. Like-minded travel companions are extremely valuable, and if they happen to also have "heartfelt unity" among them, their progress will be all the faster. Heartfelt unity implies they are not jealous of one another's progress and do not wish for each other's failure; on the contrary, they rejoice in each other's success, even if it is self-imposed. Most importantly, they must eliminate any thought of

and/or a true and virtuous guide. He inspires us when it comes to making the right choices, or sends us signs in our daily life to warn and guide us. If necessary, He may also give us a providential nudge to awaken our soul. It is enough for the driver to be attentive and to have sufficiently developed his or her sound reason to be able to correctly grasp and interpret the inspirations and signs coming from Him. In any event, He will direct our destiny in such a way as to ultimately be to our benefit.

As for those who dismiss outright any notion of God, the soul, and an accounting, or, worse, who knowingly and intentionally combat the Truth and *living real divine truths* by actively denigrating them, it could be said that their ego, driven by their imperious self, has assumed exclusive control of the wheel. The imperious self thus leads them wherever it desires, ultimately plunging them into the "ravine of ignorance"—ignorance of the Truth and divine truths—which is among the harshest torments for the human soul. The Truth is the One, and every Truth stems from Him.

---

coveting one another, be it financially or sexually. The presence of either of these on a spiritual path is a clear sign of it being misguided.

Chapter 18

And God?

He exists.
If we believe in His existence, it will be to
our own benefit; if we do not believe in His
existence, it will be to our own detriment.

O ur relationship with that which we refer to as God, and His relationship in turn with the whole of creation—the material universe (the "cosmoses") and the spiritual universes (the "heavens")—rests upon the foundational principles of gravitation, opposites, causality, etc.[1] This relationship is established and maintained through the divine flux, which is imbued with the thought, power, and will of the One. The divine flux envelops all beings: it is thus present everywhere and in everything, fulfilling the same function for beings as God's own presence. As long as human beings do not correctly grasp the equations that govern the bilateral relationship between God and His beings, and do not feel they are truly engaged in this relationship, spirituality will remain ambiguous and fictitious to them and they will be unable to grasp the real meaning of their existence. As such, they become entangled in a vicious cycle of endless objections directed toward God, the ways of the world and its inequalities, etc. Unable to find convincing answers

---

1. See chap. 1.

to their objections—which is to be expected given their mindset—they ultimately turn their backs on God. But who has more to lose here, God or human beings?

The "God" referred to here is quite distinct from the common notion of God to which an increasing number of people are becoming allergic and from which they are turning away. He is the One, the original God, pure Essence and invisible, unique and without equal. The true historical Gods,[2] who are the main links in the *chain of Divine guidance* (the authentic monotheistic religions), all emanate from the One (the original God) and are merged in Him. With every new era and epoch, each of them established a true monotheistic religion for the ethical and spiritual education of human beings (as well as those endowed with reason and free will on countless other planets) based on the foundational principles cited above. In other words, they can be likened to "mirrors" that had reflected—and continue to reflect—the thought, power, and will of the One for all beings. If humanity were to grasp the *Point of Unicity* (the tangible One), no ambiguity or duality would remain, and there would be unity in worship of the One.

Humanity's great error from the outset is to have established a mercantile relationship with God: Due to the limitations of their

---

2. The true historical Gods are not separate from the One; they are merged in Him. Accordingly, those who place their faith in the God of one of the authentic religions in this world are in direct contact with the Source of Truth (the One); as such, there is no basis for disagreement among them, for they all worship the One and are moving in the same direction. As for those who do not believe in God or in any of the religions, if they sincerely act in accordance with the voice of their conscience and the principles of humanity, and become a source of beneficence for others, the Creator will take them by the hand and guide them, eventually acquainting them with the true God, whether in this world or in the interworld.

thinking and the harsh and precarious conditions of life, they primarily sought Him to secure material benefits, unconditionally resolve their day-to-day difficulties, and ensure access to a paradise that would appeal to their ego. An even greater mistake is to have neglected and gradually all but forgotten their *essential duty* in this world, which is to engage in the process of spiritual perfection. Indeed, the majority of believers today are unaware of the fact that the essential reason for their presence on earth (the presence of their soul in a physical body) is solely to complete the fundamental stage in their process of spiritual perfection.

The majority of the faithful consider God as an all-powerful and merciful source who is in need of worship. Unconsciously, they view Him as a kind of universal problem-solver: By virtue of placing their faith in Him, worshipping Him, and making offerings to Him, He is expected to provide for their material needs, relieve their suffering, resolve their difficulties, protect their loved ones and possessions, defeat and humiliate their enemies, cure their illnesses, help them to always succeed in life, forgive their faults on demand, and, upon death, lead them to paradise. And when they no longer feel such needs within them, they forget God and turn their backs on Him. Still others see Him as an omnipotent yet exacting, wrathful, and vengeful being who is to be feared. In reality, people in each successive generation have projected their own desires onto Him according to their circumstances, such that over time each community and religion has fashioned its own version of God, even though God is but one. As for those who do not believe in God, their reasoning is as follows: "If God exists, let Him reveal Himself," which attests to their complete lack of insight into divine grandeur and humankind's insignificance.

What is being introduced here as the One is an entirely different concept of God. In the process of soundly developing our thought, we first acquaint ourselves with Him by name before coming to better know Him through His attributes. We then gradually develop an attachment to Him, such that we can no longer do without Him and cannot help but to sincerely love Him.

The One is the Source of existence and of all that is good: *All the good that befalls us is from Him.* He is the God of all, and does not belong to any one people or race. He is entirely without need or weakness. He is all-powerful, extremely generous and benevolent, yet equitable too; equitable in the sense that in His relations with beings at all strata of creation—whether in this world or the other world, in the material domain or the spiritual domain—He abides by the foundational principles that He Himself has established. His relationship with human beings is such that by virtue of His generosity, He is extremely forgiving, yet His forgiveness does not extend to those who have not made the slightest of efforts to acquire this merit. This same generosity has likewise led Him to always make *Divine guidance* available on earth for the instruction of human beings, and to place at their disposal all the means necessary to undertake their process of spiritual perfection and reach total bliss; that is the sum and substance of His obligation toward human beings. He has granted them reason and free will, leaving them free to choose whether to seek *Divine guidance* and to engage in their process of spiritual perfection or not—that is the true meaning of free will.[3]

---

3. Traditionally, there are two opposing views when it comes to philosophical discussions on determinism and free will. Proponents of absolute determinism (or fatalism) assert that everything that occurs within the realm of human existence is determined and decided by God, whereas proponents of absolute

As long as even a single being with reason and free will remains on an inhabited planet, *Divine guidance* will be accessible there, for the presence of such guidance is one of the legitimate creational rights of every being endowed with reason and free will. Let us remember that the principal responsibility of *Divine guidance* is to teach us how to soundly develop our thought on the basis of *living real divine truths*. Yet to benefit from this creational right, it falls upon us to actively and diligently seek *Divine guidance* and to connect ourselves to it—whether by means of our thought, or, better yet, with the added element of physical interaction—and to practice *in vivo* the *living real divine truths* it sets forth. It is in this manner that we can soundly develop our thought and advance in our process of spiritual perfection.

Engaging in the process of spiritual perfection is the *essential duty* of every human being. By referring to "duty," the implication is that we should not rely on another to compel us into action; no one will do so. If we invest in our process of spiritual perfection, we ourselves will benefit, and if not, we alone will endure the shame. The One will not allow us access to any of the promised "heavens" without us first having acquired the requisite spiritual acceptability here on earth. That is because by virtue of the foundational principles of gravitation and acceptability, we have not aligned the gravitational affinity of our soul with that of the heavens we seek to join in order for them to accept us. At the same time, God is not so petty as to inflict punishment or exact vengeance; rather,

---

free will assert that everything that occurs within the realm of human existence is dependent upon free will, and that God does not intervene. In reality, human beings must make their own choices within the limits of their reason and free will; in situations that exceed the limits of their free will, it is God who decides. Ostad Elahi, *Āsār ol-Haqq*, vol. 1, saying 1150.

it is the consequences of our own actions that come back to us. In other words, it is the "embodiment" of our own wrongful acts that torments us in the hereafter;[4] this torment will not cease until such time as He has forgiven us.

As for divine forgiveness, we must not repeat the grave error of our ancestors in confounding the forgiveness of our wrongdoings ("sins") with reaching spiritual perfection. The generosity of the One is so great that He will eventually forgive everyone in one way or another, but to reach Perfection (total bliss), we ourselves must acquire the requisite *spiritual acceptability*. And this spiritual acceptability is realized through the *in vivo* practice of *living real divine truths*, truths that are understood through the sound development of one's thought. Engaging in the process of spiritual perfection through the sound development of one's thought can be likened to earning academic credits at a university. Divine forgiveness is akin to allowing a student who repeatedly fails a class—as a result of laziness or the pursuit of other distractions—to reenroll despite his or her failings. While this allowance enables the student to remain enrolled instead of being expelled, it does not substitute for the credits required to pass. The student must still complete the coursework and pass the required examinations. Similarly, Perfection implies that a

---

4. "What need does God have to inflict wrath? That which people perceive as His wrath is none other than the reflection of their own actions that surrounds them. God is compassionate and munificent. If we are faced with any wrath, it is not from Him that it originates, but simply the reaction to our own actions." (Ostad Elahi, *Paroles de Vérité*, saying 89) We can understand divine wrath in the following way: If the wrongful acts of a being endowed with reason are such as to bring about this wrath, it would still require God's consent—as would any other occurrence—before it can come to pass. In any event, no action remains without a reaction.

spiritual student has successfully passed all the theoretical and practical tests (trials) and obtained a "doctorate" (i.e., has come to know the divine spark within), and has advanced his or her studies to reach a "professorship" (Perfection).

We should not expect our soul to spontaneously and naturally develop and advance toward its maturity, as is the case with our physical body. The development and maturity of our soul occurs in parallel with the development and maturity of our sound reason, and it is up to each of us to attain this maturity through the sound development of our thought. If we do not nourish our soul with *living real divine truths* (the building blocks for the sound development of thought), neither our sound reason, nor in turn our soul, will develop, and we will remain spiritually weak and ineffectual. Furthermore, the souls of those who also persist in committing wrongful acts may in time come to exceptionally lose their *divine spark* and transform into worthless "residue" (Fig. 6).

In summary, anyone who sincerely seeks the Truth will be connected to *Divine guidance* by the Creator. Thereafter, it is our own duty to take advantage of this connection, practice *in vivo* the *living real divine truths* that such guidance sets forth, and pass the corresponding tests so that we can gradually come to know our real self (our soul) and to know God. It is within ourselves and through our own soul that we must come to see and know God; such self-knowledge constitutes a critical stage in the process of reaching Perfection.

We should bear in mind that the original nature of the soul, its ultimate purpose, and the *living real divine truths* that are the building blocks for the sound development of one's thought are immutable, such that the passage of time has no effect on them. What changes is only the manner in which these truths are presented and applied, as well as the intellectual aptitude of beings endowed with reason and free will. All of us will ultimately return to the hereafter with the same self, the same self-consciousness, and the same "mental baggage" that we had acquired on earth. After spending several or more lifetimes here,[5] it is in that other world (the hereafter) that we will forever remain, where we will know neither death nor forgetfulness: Death pertains to the physical body, not to the soul (our real self), and forgetfulness pertains to the brain, not to the metabrain. If, during these limited sojourns to earth, we do not take any positive steps to secure our life in the hereafter and instead spend our time and energy on futile and ephemeral pursuits, then by virtue of the foundational principles of gravitation, causality, acceptability, etc., our circumstances in the hereafter will leave much to be desired. Indeed, we will find ourselves in a state of confusion, "illiteracy," helplessness, humiliation, and regret, while knowing full well that we alone are responsible for our plight; we are aware that during our life on earth we placed ourselves entirely at the disposal of our ego—especially our imperious self—and took notions such as God, the soul, life in the hereafter, and an accounting to be illusory and risible.

In the end, if there were but a single attribute of the One we should cement in our mind, it would be His generosity. We must always retain hope in His generosity, which is such that if we were to practice and assimilate even a single *living real divine truth* within our soul during our

---

5. For more on the subject of ascending successive lives, see Ostad Elahi, *Ma'refat ol-Ruh*, 119; B. Elahi, *La Voie de la Perfection,* chap. 8.

life on earth, He would use that as both a pretext and a hook to rescue us from the pit of spiritual ignorance and set us on the right path.

Chapter 19

Recommendation

The whole of creation can be thought of as a megaorganism whose constituent parts—from the smallest (elementary particles . . .) to the largest (the cosmoses, the planets, the heavens . . .)—rest upon the foundational principles[1] established by the original God (the One). Creation is governed by the divine flux—the flux of consciousness of the One—which envelops and penetrates all beings, without exception. As such, all beings throughout creation are simultaneously in direct contact with the One, just as He is simultaneously in direct contact with each and every one of them.

All of us can tangibly grasp and experience these foundational principles in our own lives, especially the principles of gravitation, causality, and opposites. For instance, if creation were not rooted in divine gravitation, there would be no faith, love, or hatred; without the order in creation induced by causality, there would be no science; and without the principle of opposites, no knowledge could be realized. The same holds true for the principle of connection: If we want to become a physicist or a physician, for instance, we must first apply (and be accepted) to an accredited university and complete the requisite coursework that has been established for that discipline. We would then have to take

---

1. These foundational principles include gravitation, opposites, causality, legitimate rights, connection, *in vivo* practice, acceptability, Divine generosity, and exception. See chap. 1.

and successfully pass the tests specific to that discipline. Likewise, if our goal in spirituality is to complete the fundamental stage in our process of spiritual perfection, we must—in accordance with the principle of connection—connect to *Divine guidance* by way of our thought, apply in an *in vivo* manner the *living real divine truths* it sets forth, and then undergo and pass the corresponding tests, which pertain to our character weak points and flaws relating to divine or ethical principles. Without such a connection to *Divine guidance*, we will not know what constitutes true spirituality nor what spiritual goal to follow; we will not know which actions to avoid and which ones to pursue, and in particular how to go about doing so. As such, it is all but certain that we will find ourselves confused and lost in our process of spiritual perfection.

Any spirituality whose goal is to lead one's soul toward Perfection must be approached as an experimental science, meaning as a process that is based on the *sound development of one's thought*. This process concerns, without exception, all beings endowed with reason and free will, including human beings. It must be undertaken with utmost resolve, for it pertains to our real self (our soul), which continues its existence perpetually and knows no death—it is only our physical body that dies, not our soul. Each time we die, we leave our physical body behind and temporarily enter the interworld specific to our own planet. The sound development of our thought renders our soul (our real self) attentive and active, enables us to examine and mend our faith, and helps us to develop our sound reason so that with the help of such faith and sound reason, we can come to also cultivate our humanity while we are still here on earth.

From a spiritual standpoint, as long as we are here on this earth, we have but one *essential duty*: to complete the fundamental stage in our process of spiritual perfection. Toward that end, we must engage in the sound development of our thought so that we do not find ourselves weak, ignorant, disoriented, and helpless in the hereafter, reduced to mendicity. Life in this world is necessary and of great value to our spiritual destiny, for in principle it is only on earth that we can complete the fundamental stage in our process of spiritual perfection. Once we have completed this stage here on earth, we no longer need to return to this world of spiritual amnesia, of deception and conflict. No longer will we have to endure anew the difficulties and pressures of earthly life, but instead will be allowed (admitted) to remain in the interworld where we can potentially complete the advanced stage in our process of spiritual perfection.

Accordingly, it is strongly advisable that we not neglect the spiritual side of our life and avoid squandering our precious time on futile pursuits. In particular, those who are about to engage in spirituality, as well as those who already adhere to a religion or spiritual path, are cautioned to avoid following a guide that is devoid of the Essence[2] or a guidance that is not designated by the Source of Truth (the One). Indeed, the principles imparted by such a guide or guidance lack any *divine effect* and are thus spiritually defunct and sterile. The practice of these principles not only fails to benefit the soul (it does not develop one's sound reason), but actually reinforces one's ego and imperious self, leading to the soul's corruption. It is therefore far healthier for one to remain an atheist without a professed religion or spiritual belief—provided one strives to be beneficent and not cause anyone harm—than to follow the prescriptions of a false religion and/or to place one's faith in a god that is

---

2. See chap. 3.

untrue. Such a person's accounting in the hereafter will also prove to be more favorable.

As the majority of people are spiritually amnesic and do not receive a correct spiritual education, they are frequently mistaken in their choice of a spiritual path and guide. At the present time,[3] the only solution is to wholeheartedly and sincerely entrust themselves to the Creator and to request His help in choosing a correct path for them. Indeed, regardless of their beliefs, the Creator has made it incumbent upon Himself to connect to *Divine guidance* those who *sincerely seek the Truth*—even if such sincerity is self-imposed—and to not allow them to fall prey to the false religions and misguided spiritual paths that abound.

What is Meant by "Truth"?

"Truth" here refers to several things: (1) the absolute Truth (the One), the Source of Truth from which all Truths emanate; (2) the true historical Gods, who bear the thought, power, and will of the One (such as the Gods of the authentic monotheistic religions); (3) the truth of one's being, which is one's soul; (4) the truth of one's faith—that it be directed toward the One or a true God; (5) the truth of a spiritual path—that it set forth a process for developing one's sound reason by way of the sound development of one's thought; and (6) *living real divine truths* (which include correct divine and ethical principles)— prescriptions, theoretical and practical, issued by the Source of Truth (the One) that bear the divine effect (i.e., they are living) and are intended to soundly develop the thought of beings endowed with reason and free will, including human beings.

---

3. In the future, it is certain that in spirituality, as in every other domain of knowledge, we will be able to discern truth from falsehood with the help of science and technology.

Chapter 20

A Few Key Practical Points

We cannot elude death, but it is our physical body that dies, not our real self (our soul). We will live forever with this same self in the spiritual dimensions—one that is commensurate with the level of advancement achieved by our soul while here on earth. Whether we live our life in eternal bliss or misery depends on how we choose to apply our free will. The only way that we can achieve a higher level for our soul and live in bliss in the hereafter is through the *in vivo* practice of *living real divine truths* set forth by *Divine guidance*.

We should engrave the following principle in our consciousness: Life in this world is an invaluable asset for the education and development of our soul, and must not be squandered on futile pursuits. Futile pursuits are thoughts and actions that contribute nothing positive to our life in this world or in the other. We should remember that this earthly world is in principle the only place that we can undertake the fundamental stage in our process of spiritual perfection. Thus, the reason for our presence—the presence of our soul—on this earth within a human body is to complete the fundamental stage in our process of spiritual perfection. Completing the fundamental stage here affords us the great advantage of acquiring the acceptability to remain in the interworld upon our return so that we can continue and potentially conclude—under far better conditions in its "learning institutions"—the advanced stage in our process of spiritual perfection in order to reach Perfection.

The fundamental stage can be summarized in three main points: (1) examining and mending our faith, (2) sufficiently developing our sound reason, and (3) cultivating our humanity.

1) How Can We Examine and Mend Our Faith?

We can examine and mend our faith by exercising as much diligence as necessary to ensure that we are placing our faith in a true God—for example, the God of one of the authentic monotheistic religions, such as the God of Abraham, the God of Zoroaster, the entity that illuminated the historical Buddha, the God of Moses, the God of Christ, the God of Muhammad—or directly in the One Himself (the original God) or in the *Point of Unicity*. Such a faith can be considered a "correct" faith. Given that all true Gods originate from and are merged in the One, by addressing a true God, it is as if we were addressing the One. Recall that no one can reach Perfection without the steadfast support of the metacausal energy of the One, and that such energy can only be acquired through faith in a true God.

2) How Can We Develop Our Sound Reason?

When we make it a habit to align our daily comportment (intentions and actions) with the voice of our conscience and divine contentment, we will automatically enable the conditions for a state of *constant attention*. Such a state of attention does not in any way disrupt the normal course of our life. Until this state of constant attention becomes second nature to us, an effective exercise to develop it is to regularly recall that the One, by way of the divine flux, is always present and observant. Constant attention to God enables us to absorb Divine light on a daily basis and in a natural (physiological) dose that avoids inducing altered states of consciousness. Divine light bears metacausal energy and confers the discernment of Truth. Metacausal energy renders our soul awake and active, whereas the inoculation of our soul with the discernment of Truth develops our sound reason. When our sound reason reaches a sufficient level of development and a rational love of Truth emerges within us, our focus will then spontaneously shift from futile material and spiritual pursuits to *living real divine truths*, and we will naturally aspire to practice them. Thereafter, the more we practice these *living real divine truths* in an *in vivo* manner, the more we will develop our sound reason. It should be noted that the development of one's soul is measured by the development of one's sound reason.

In addition, the daily exercise of attention-dialogue—once or several times throughout the day, for a few minutes or more on each occasion—is extremely effective in developing one's constant attention.

3) How Can We Cultivate Our Humanity?

We must begin by turning our constant attention into a state of perfect attention—that is, at the same time that our attention is constantly directed toward God, we must also monitor the spiritually harmful activities of our imperious self in order to prevent the latter from harming our soul. Next, we must strive in our daily life to put ourselves in the place of others, doing unto them that we which we want and do for ourselves, while that which we avoid and consider as harmful for ourselves, we likewise deem harmful for others and shield them from it to the extent possible. "Others" in the first instance refers to our fellow beings, and then to animals, plants, nature, and even objects. Given that each being bears a consciousness specific to its own group and level, and thereby enjoys its own rights, humanity makes it incumbent upon us to respect these rights to the extent possible (including those of our own). "When we want for others what we consider as good for ourselves and act accordingly, we have become truly human, and the virtues of humanity naturally emanate from us."[1] In practice, it is with the help of a "correct" faith and a sufficiently developed sound reason that we can come to cultivate our humanity and thereby complete the fundamental stage in our process of spiritual perfection in this world.

Accordingly, the process of spiritual perfection can be summarized as follows: With the use of our willpower and steadfast support from the metacausal energy of the One, we must (1) identify each of the psychospiritual forces that are in functional disequilibrium within us (our character weak points and flaws relating to divine or ethical principles), and (2) gradually control them until they acquire the acceptability to be transmuted into divine virtues by the One, such that they become integrated into our soul's genetic makeup and remain permanently with us.

The process of spiritual perfection is extremely precise and can be likened to a chemical equation: Without the steadfast support of the metacausal energy of the One, no one can overcome the imperious self and advance in the process of spiritual perfection; likewise, without sound reason, no one can correctly grasp the spiritual dimension of life, for common reason lacks the capacity to do so. In this equation, the two indispensable elements (reagents) are the metacausal energy of the

---

1. Ostad Elahi, *Paroles de Vérité*, saying 27.

One and sound reason. Without either of these two elements, it is all but certain that we would stagnate or stray in the process of spiritual perfection and could not reach our destination.

At the outset, strong willpower and perseverance are needed to bring ourselves to pursue our process of spiritual perfection. But if the God in whom we have placed our faith is true, the more we gradually assimilate *living real divine truths*, the more our sound reason will develop and the more our rational love of Truth will increase. If we remain steadfast, we will reach a point of becoming accustomed to fighting the imperious self and will naturally develop a propensity for it. The rational love of Truth, together with hope and confidence in our future, will thus come to permeate our entire being, and we will continue to progress with enthusiasm and perseverance until we reach Perfection.

Epilogue

Based on the words and writings[1] that remain from Ostad, we can conclude the following:

The One *was* and there existed none other. Out of His generosity, He willed to bestow total bliss (eternal felicity).[2] By virtue of this will and from the radiance of the One, the *Quiddity-Matter* came to be, from which the Quiddity, and then souls of various types, natures, levels, and capacities, as well as corporealities—lifeless and motionless—came into existence. Upon His command, groups of souls gradually entered—and continue to enter—corporealities specific to their own kind, infusing them with transubstantial movement, development, life, and consciousness. The "world"[3] was set into motion and creatures—in different groups, with varying natures, levels, capacities for consciousness, and innate aptitudes—were thus created and continue to be created.

---

1. In particular, a manuscript entitled *Kashf ol-Haqāyeq*, a segment of which has been translated into French and can be found in B. Elahi, *La Voie de la Perfection*, 219-26.
2. Based on His generosity and equity, we can assume that the metacausal ecstasy of one who has reached Perfection is experienced by that person's entire being; that is, in addition to the celestial soul, the totality of the mineral, vegetal, and animal souls that had merged with this celestial soul during its process of spiritual perfection (and whose quintessential properties the celestial soul had absorbed and integrated) also experience such a state.
3. "World" here refers to the whole of creation.

Every being is endowed with a "soul," which confers upon it a "consciousness"[4] and "comprehension" specific to its own kind. Each being's capacity for consciousness and comprehension is commensurate with its level on the evolutionary continuum of beings; this capacity is greatest in the human soul. The goal of creation is for all beings to ascend the steps in the process of spiritual perfection so that they can ultimately come to enjoy total bliss. Toward that end, every being, from the moment of its appearance in the material world, is immediately enmeshed within nature's causal chain; overseen by the One and through natural determinism, it then evolves—in body and soul—until its consciousness has reached such a level as to acquire the aptitude to merge with and dissolve within the soul of a being endowed with reason (here, a human being), while preserving its quintessential properties.

For beings endowed with reason and thereby free will, the One, through the intermediary of His messengers, brings them to understand their ultimate goal (Perfection), as well as the prescriptions and proscriptions they must observe in order to achieve that goal. He also places at their disposal all the means necessary for their spiritual perfection. As such, all that remains for beings endowed with reason and free will (including human beings) is to engage in the *essential duty*[5] of undertaking their process of spiritual perfection. Those who are able to fulfill this essential duty and engage in their process of spiritual perfection—by means of their own willpower and effort,

---

4. The most basic level of "consciousness" pertains to minerals (or lower still), while the most complete and developed level pertains to human beings.

5. "During the course of its existence, it is the duty of every being, to the extent of its understanding and physical ability, and free of unbearable constraints or inordinate impositions, to strive and endeavor to traverse the stages of its process of spiritual perfection." Ostad Elahi, *Ma'refat ol-Ruh*, 57.

and with steadfast support from the metacausal energy of the One—until their knowledge of Truth is complete will reach *the threshold of Perfection*. But crossing this threshold and reaching Perfection are solely dependent upon His will. Those who reach Perfection by the will of the One acquire the acceptability to merge, like a drop of pure water, with the *Ocean of Truth*; preserving their self-consciousness and with full lucidity, they join one of the levels of Perfection[6]—commensurate with the station and capacity of their soul—where, overflowing with metacausal love for the One, they will forever remain in total bliss.

From the "moment" that the One willed, a very . . . very . . . long time had passed. The One still remained imperceptible to beings, even to those who had reached the highest level of Perfection. He chose the highest among them, who once again assumed a human body and traversed "the process of perfection within Perfection" until no weak point remained in its "soul" and it had acquired the pure quality of the Essence. It then merged with the One, as if becoming one with Him, and the *Point of Unicity* (the tangible One) thus appeared. It is such that the One, through the *Point of Unicity*, rendered Himself perceptible and tangible to beings.

---

6. "As the Origin of each person differs, so does his or her Return, each making the Return at his or her own level." (*Âsâr ol-Haqq*, vol. 2, 277) Perfection, too, has different levels. Given that the capacity for comprehension and the spiritual station of human souls vary, so too does the level they come to occupy within Perfection. Yet regardless of the level a human soul occupies within Perfection, its cup of bliss is full, and it doesn't desire to be anything other than what it is. See Ostad Elahi, *Paroles de Vérité*, saying 413.

Select Bibliography

Elahi, Ostad (Nur Ali). *Āsār ol-Haqq*. Compiled and edited by Bahram Elahi. Vol. 1. 5ᵗʰ ed. Tehran: Nashr-e Panj, 2007.

———. *Āsār ol-Haqq*. Compiled and edited by Bahram Elahi. Vol. 2. 2d ed. Tehran: Jeyhun, 1994.

———. *Bargozideh: Gozide-ye az Goftārhā-ye Nur Ali Elahi*. Compiled and edited by Bahram Elahi. Tehran: Nashr-e Panj, 2008. Translated by Leili Anvar under the title *Paroles de Vérité* (Paris: Albin Michel, 2014).

———. *Borhān ol-Haqq*. 8ᵗʰ ed. Tehran: Jeyhun, 1994.

———. Commentary on *Haqq ol-Haqāyeq* (*Shāhnāme-ye Haqiqat*), by Hādj Nematollāh Jeyhunābādi. Tehran: Jeyhun, 1994.

———. *Kashf ol-Haqāyeq*. Unpublished manuscript, 1923.

———. *Madjma ol-Kalām*. Unpublished manuscript, 1922.

———. *Ma'refat ol-Ruh*. 4ᵗʰ ed. Tehran: Jeyhun, 2000. Translated by James W. Morris under the title *Knowing the Spirit* (New York: State University of New York Press, 2007).

———. *Words of Faith: Prayers of Ostad Elahi*. Edited by Bahram Elahi. Paris: Robert Laffont, 1995.